Christian Jr./Sr High School
2100 Greenfield Dr
El Cajon, CA 92019

DATE DUE

#47-0108 Peel Off Pressure Sensitive

COMPREHENSIVE RESEARCH
AND STUDY GUIDE

BLOOM'S
MAJOR
SHORT
STORY
WRITERS

Flannery
O'Connor

EDITED AND WITH AN
INTRODUCTION BY HAROLD BLOOM

Christian Jr./Sr High School
2100 Greenfield Dr
El Cajon. CA 92010

CURRENTLY AVAILABLE

BLOOM'S MAJOR DRAMATISTS

Anton Chekhov
Henrik Ibsen
Arthur Miller
Eugene O'Neill
Shakespeare's Comedies
Shakespeare's Histories
Shakespeare's Romances
Shakespeare's Tragedies
George Bernard Shaw
Tennessee Williams

BLOOM'S MAJOR NOVELISTS

Jane Austen
The Brontës
Willa Cather
Charles Dickens
William Faulkner
F. Scott Fitzgerald
Nathaniel Hawthorne
Ernest Hemingway
Toni Morrison
John Steinbeck
Mark Twain
Alice Walker

BLOOM'S MAJOR SHORT STORY WRITERS

William Faulkner
F. Scott Fitzgerald
Ernest Hemingway
O. Henry
James Joyce
Herman Melville
Flannery O'Connor
Edgar Allan Poe
J. D. Salinger
John Steinbeck
Mark Twain
Eudora Welty

BLOOM'S MAJOR WORLD POETS

Geoffrey Chaucer
Emily Dickinson
John Donne
T. S. Eliot
Robert Frost
Langston Hughes
John Milton
Edgar Allan Poe
Shakespeare's Poems & Sonnets
Alfred, Lord Tennyson
Walt Whitman
William Wordsworth

BLOOM'S NOTES

The Adventures of Huckleberry Finn
Aeneid
The Age of Innocence
Animal Farm
The Autobiography of Malcolm X
The Awakening
Beloved
Beowulf
Billy Budd, Benito Cereno, & Bartleby the Scrivener
Brave New World
The Catcher in the Rye
Crime and Punishment
The Crucible

Death of a Salesman
A Farewell to Arms
Frankenstein
The Grapes of Wrath
Great Expectations
The Great Gatsby
Gulliver's Travels
Hamlet
Heart of Darkness & The Secret Sharer
Henry IV, Part One
I Know Why the Caged Bird Sings
Iliad
Inferno
Invisible Man
Jane Eyre
Julius Caesar

King Lear
Lord of the Flies
Macbeth
A Midsummer Night's Dream
Moby-Dick
Native Son
Nineteen Eighty-Four
Odyssey
Oedipus Plays
Of Mice and Men
The Old Man and the Sea
Othello
Paradise Lost
A Portrait of the Artist as a Young Man
The Portrait of a Lady

Pride and Prejudice
The Red Badge of Courage
Romeo and Juliet
The Scarlet Letter
Silas Marner
The Sound and the Fury
The Sun Also Rises
A Tale of Two Cities
Tess of the D'Urbervilles
Their Eyes Were Watching God
To Kill a Mockingbird
Uncle Tom's Cabin
Wuthering Heights

COMPREHENSIVE RESEARCH
AND STUDY GUIDE

BLOOM'S
M A J O R
SHORT STORY
W R I T E R S

Flannery
O'Connor

Christian Jr./Sr High School
2100 Greenfield Dr
El Cajon, CA 92019

© 1999 by Chelsea House Publishers, a Subsidiary of Haights Cross Communications.

Introduction © 1999 by Harold Bloom

All rights reserved. No part of this publication may be reproduced or transmitted in any form or by any means without the written permission of the publisher.

Printed and bound in the United States of America.

3 5 7 9 8 6 4

Library of Congress Cataloging-in-Publication Data
Flannery O'Connor edited and with an introduction by Harold Bloom.
p.   cm. – (Bloom's major short story writers)
Includes bibliographical references and index.
ISBN 0-7910-5119-6 (hc)
O'Connor, Flannery—Criticism and interpretation—Handbooks,
Manuals, etc.   2. Women and literature—Southern States—History—
20th century.   3. O'Connor, Flannery—Examinations—Study guides—
4. Short story—Examinations—Study guides.   5. Short story—
Handbooks, manuals, etc.   I. Bloom, Harold.   II. Series.
PS3565.C57Z66783 1998
813'.54—dc21
98-31662
CIP

Chelsea House Publishers
1974 Sproul Road, Suite 400
Broomall, PA 19008-0914

CONTRIBUTING EDITOR: Aaron Tillman

Contents

User's Guide

This volume is designed to present biographical, critical, and bibliographical information on the author's best-known or most important short stories. Following Harold Bloom's editor's note and introduction is a detailed biography of the author, discussing major life events and important literary accomplishments. A plot summary of each short story follows, tracing significant themes, patterns, and motifs in the work, and an annotated list of characters supplies brief information on the main characters in each story.

A selection of critical extracts, derived from previously published material from leading critics, analyzes aspects of each short story. The extracts consist of statements from the author, if available, early reviews of the work, and later evaluations up to the present. A bibliography of the author's writings (including a complete list of all books written, cowritten, edited, and translated), a list of additional books and articles on the author and the work, and an index of themes and ideas in the author's writings conclude the volume.

~

Harold Bloom is Sterling Professor of the Humanities at Yale University and Henry W. and Albert A. Berg Professor of English at the New York University Graduate School. He is the author of over 20 books and the editor of more than 30 anthologies of literary criticism.

Professor Bloom's works include *Shelley's Mythmaking* (1959), *The Visionary Company* (1961), *Blake's Apocalypse* (1963), *Yeats* (1970), *A Map of Misreading* (1975), *Kabbalah and Criticism* (1975), and *Agon: Toward a Theory of Revisionism* (1982). *The Anxiety of Influence* (1973) sets forth Professor Bloom's provocative theory of the literary relationships between the great writers and their predecessors. His most recent books include *The American Religion* (1992), *The Western Canon* (1994), *Omens of Millennium: The Gnosis of Angels, Dreams, and Resurrection* (1996), and *Shakespeare: The Invention of the Human* (1998).

Professor Bloom earned his Ph.D. from Yale University in 1955 and has served on the Yale faculty since then. He is a 1985 MacArthur Foundation Award recipient and served as the Charles Eliot Norton Professor of Poetry at Harvard University in 1987–88. He is currently the editor of other Chelsea House series in literary criticism, including BLOOM'S NOTES, BLOOM'S MAJOR POETS, MAJOR LITERARY CHARACTERS, MODERN CRITICAL VIEWS, MODERN CRITICAL INTERPRETATIONS, and WOMEN WRITERS OF ENGLISH AND THEIR WORKS.

Editor's Note

My Introduction examines some of the perplexities evoked by Flannery O'Connor's rather fierce stance towards some of the protagonists in her stories.

Critical Views on "A Good Man Is Hard to Find" begin with Father Gardiner's praise of O'Connor's lack of sentimentality, and continue with Irving Malin's account of the story's images of the "horror of self-love." Frederick J. Hoffmann sees O'Connor as a writer who shocks us into accepting the validity of religion, while Claire Kahane analyzes O'Connor's remarkable attention to details. A startling comparison of the Misfit to Job is made by Ruthann Knechel Johansen, after which Robert H. Brinkmeyer, Jr. traces elements in O'Connor's imaginative sympathy with Southern Fundamentalism.

"Good Country People" is judged by Robert Drake to be one of O'Connor's prime protests against modernist "enlightenment," while C. Hugh Holman sees the story as a consequence of the writer's Southern Agrarian "rage for order." To Dorothy Tuck McFarland, the tale's characters are trapped in meaningless platitudes, after which Anthony Di Renzo praises the ribaldry of O'Connor's art. A feminist perspective is provided by Jeanne Campbell Reesman, while Joanne Halleran McMullen explores ironies in the writer's detachment from her own theological concerns.

"Everything that Rises Must Converge" is for Carter W. Martin a parable of redemption, but for Preston M. Browning, Jr. it is a condemnation of Julian's bad faith. The contrast between whites and blacks in the story is emphasized by Janet Egleson Dunleavy, after which Edward Kessler regards Julian as being akin to a Hawthorne character, and John F. Desmond meditates upon O'Connor's attitude towards history. Marshall Bruce Gentry suggests that the typical narrator of an O'Connor story is a woman who espouses male and patriarchal values.

"Revelation" is judged by Sister M. Bernetta Quinn to be "realistic," while for Ronald Schleifer the story is rather one of Gothic symbolism. Michael Gresset wonders at the story's relation to faith, while the formidable Richard Poirier rightly sees pride as being the sin that O'Connor never forgives.

Jill P. Baumgaertner examines the extremity of the writer's vision, after which Patricia Yaeger is tempted "to rewrite O'Connor's tortured texts as angry feminist legends."

Introduction

HAROLD BLOOM

An exemplary Catholic in her overt faith, Flannery O'Connor wrote out of so profound an apprehension of her country's indigenous religion that perhaps only Faulkner, in the century now ending, gives us an equally intense vision of American spirituality. The Faulkner of *As I Lay Dying* and *Light in August* is the literary father of O'Connor's *Complete Stories* and *The Violent Bear It Away*. Though normative Christian critics, like the late Cleanth Brooks, have baptized Faulkner's imagination, the seer of the Bundrens and the Compsons had accepted no revelation of Christianity. Publicly, O'Connor was ardent in proclaiming Original Sin and the Fall, but I trust the tales and not their teller. Her greatest stories do not show us grace correcting nature, but rather a condition in which everything fell precisely as and when it was created. The American Religion—an original but unstable blend of Orphism, gnosticism, and Enthusiasm—is as powerfully portrayed by O'Connor as by any other of our storytellers, from Hawthorne to Cormac McCarthy.

I recall being denounced by one of my former students, a pious person, for having characterized O'Connor's fictions as being essentially Gnostic, despite her Catholic convictions. But my denouncer misunderstood her art, which has its own life apart from her faith. It is not accidental that O'Connor's favorite novels were Faulkner's *As I Lay Dying* and Nathanael West's *Miss Lonelyhearts*, works of an authentic nihilism. Reducing a story by O'Connor to a Catholic parable is a vain exercise; her comic mode is akin to Faulkner's and West's, and not to G.K. Chesterton's. Compassion is not one of O'Connor's prime virtues, as a writer. She was a parodist of genius (again like West) and she wisely refrained from representing her own Catholic vision, which then might have emerged as only another parody. As an artist, she had the grand fortune of being a Southern American Catholic surrounded by Fundamentalist Protestants, American Religionists who provided a perfect *materia poetica* for her. The inspired prophets among them seemed to her "natural Catholics," a judgment remarkable in its spiritual audacity, and yet it became another splendid enhancement for her art. Pride, the prime sin in her many grotesque and unsympathetic secular characters, is implicitly liberated by her when it is associated with the sacred violence of prophetic election.

Transcendence through violence is an unfortunate American mode, in life as in literature. O'Connor was too shrewd to venture upon so aesthetically self-defeating a quest, though some of her partisans fall into the error of seeing her as an apostle of grace-through-violence. Encountering transcendence seems all too easy for American religionists, but representing such encounters is quite another endeavor. John Burt catches the individuality of O'Connor's enterprise in regard to her novel, *Wise Blood:*

> O'Connor has it both ways in *Wise Blood.* She herself rejects the inward power which her characters take as their sole authority, and through irony and even ridicule she forcefully keeps her point of view separate from theirs. But at the same time this inward power seems . . . to win . . . the grudging respect of both author and reader.

O'Connor's respect for the protagonists of her best stories is sometimes grudging, and frequently ironic, where it exists at all. Her attitude towards her readers is even more complex. Fierce in her belief, O'Connor disdains our skepticism. Our representatives in the stories include the grandmother in the notorious "A Good Man Is Hard to Find," and it is perfectly accurate to observe that the Misfit speaks for something in O'Connor, when he elegizes his victim: "She would of been a good woman, if it had been somebody there to shoot her every minute of her life." Shall we not say of poor Hulga Hopewell in "Good Country People" that: "She would of been a good woman, if it had been somebody there to seduce her and run off with her wooden leg every minute of her life." Parodying Flannery O'Connor is hardly a useful critical procedure, but her incessant tendentiousness is provocative, and does not always serve the interests of her art.

No one ever is going to feel much affection for Julian, the would-be-writer in "Everything That Rises Must Converge," but he too might provoke the parodistic formula: "He would of been a good man, if it had been somebody there to strike his mother down and kill her every minute of his life." I prefer "Revelation" to the other three stories studied in this volume, precisely because its Mrs. Ruby Turpin transcends the O'Connor formula. Moved perhaps by Mrs. Turpin's courage, O'Connor grants her an authentic vision, at the close, in which she hears "the voices of the souls climbing upward and shouting hallelujah." Mrs. Turpin appears to require no further violence. ❀

Biography of
Flannery O'Connor

(1925–1964)

Mary Flannery O'Connor, the only child of Regina Cline and Edwin Francis O'Connor, was born in Savannah, Georgia, on March 25, 1925. In 1937, Edwin O'Connor developed disseminated lupus and the family moved to Milledgeville, Georgia, Regina Cline's birthplace and the home of the Cline family since before the Civil War. In 1941, Mary Flannery's father died. She lived in Milledgeville for eight years and attended Peabody High School, then Georgia State College for Women (now Georgia College). She graduated from Georgia State College for Women in 1945.

In college, Mary Flannery developed a passion for reading and writing. Her potential was recognized and rewarded with a scholarship for master's degree studies. She decided to temporarily leave her southern homestead and head northwest to attend the School for Writers, headed by Paul Engle at Iowa State University. In Iowa, she became known as Flannery O'Connor, leaving her first name behind as she had her Milledgeville home. It was in Iowa that her writing career truly began.

In 1946, while O'Connor was still a student, her first story, "The Geranium," was published in *Accent* magazine. In 1947, she received her Master's in Fine Arts from the University of Iowa. She also received the Rinehart-Iowa Fiction Award for a first novel with a portion of her then-unfinished work, *Wise Blood*. She also garnered a recommendation for a place at Yaddo writer's colony in Saratoga Springs, New York, where she lived until the spring of 1949.

From 1949 to 1950, O'Connor continued to work on completing *Wise Blood*, living briefly in New York City and then moving to Ridgefield, Connecticut, to live with the Robert Fitzgerald family. In December of 1950, Flannery O'Connor developed disseminated lupus—the same disease as her father, Edwin, had. She moved back to Georgia. In 1951, Flannery and her mother, Regina, moved to a dairy farm called "Andalusia," located five miles outside of Milledgeville. In 1952, *Wise Blood* was published.

Despite the serious physical symptoms of her illness, O'Connor remained mentally active and began working on the stories that would appear in her book *A Good Man Is Hard to Find and Other Stories.* She published them in various literary journals before collecting them in one volume. In December of 1952, she received the Kenyon Review Fellowship in Fiction, a prize sponsored by the Rockefeller Foundation. In 1955, *A Good Man Is Hard to Find and Other Stories* was published.

In the process of compiling *A Good Man Is Hard to Find*, O'Connor had also begun working on the initial chapters of what would later become her second novel, *The Violent Bear It Away.* She completed the first draft of this book in January 1959. In late 1959, she received the Ford Foundation Grant. In January 1960, *The Violent Bear It Away* was published.

Flannery O'Connor's medical condition remained relatively stable for over three years following the publication of *The Violent Bear It Away.* In the summer of 1963, she received an honorary degree from Smith College. That fall, her health began to decline.

During the weeks leading up to Christmas of 1963, O'Connor began experiencing prolonged periods of weakness coupled with increasingly frequent fainting spells. Upon receiving treatment for anemia, she began to recuperate. Her recovery seems to have spurred a burst of productivity. She wrote and revised the stories that would later appear in her last collection, *Everything That Rises Must Converge.* In February 1964, it was discovered that a fibroid tumor was the cause of her severe anemia. Although an operation on a lupus patient was a risky proposition, there were few viable alternatives. On February 25, 1964, O'Connor was admitted to Baldwin County Hospital, where she underwent surgery to remove the tumor.

Although the operation initially appeared to be a success, it was soon apparent that the surgery had exacerbated her lupus. Seemingly aware that her lifetime was coming to an end, Flannery O'Connor worked as diligently as her condition permitted to complete three more stories for her final collection: "Revelation," "Judgment Day," and "Parker's Back." On August 3, 1964, Flannery O'Connor died in Milledgeville Hospital in Milledgeville, Georgia.

In 1965, her final collection of stories, *Everything That Rises Must Converge,* was published. In 1969, a book of selected prose and essays entitled *Mystery and Manners* was published. In 1971, Flannery O'Connor's *Collected Stories* was published. This volume included all the stories contained in her two previous collections, the stories written for the fulfillment of her M.F.A. requirements, the original excerpts from both of her novels (segments of which had previously been published in story form), a portion of an uncompleted novel, and a final uncollected story. In 1972, *Collected Stories* received the National Book Award. In 1979, *The Habit of Being,* an edited selection of her letters, was published. ❀

Plot Summary of
"A Good Man Is Hard to Find"

"A Good Man Is Hard to Find," the title story of Flannery O'Connor's first collection, opens on the eve of a Georgia family's car trip to Florida. The family consists of Bailey, his wife, their three children and the grandmother, Bailey's mother, who is the central figure of the story. O'Connor's opening sentence, "The grandmother didn't want to go to Florida," immediately begins to establish her domineering nature. The grandmother attempts to persuade her son to visit relatives in east Tennessee. She tries to deter him from going to Florida by thrusting a newspaper article about an escaped felon called "The Misfit," who is apparently headed for Florida, into his face. A responsible parent wouldn't take such a risk, she says: "I wouldn't take my children in any direction with a criminal like that aloose in it. I couldn't answer to my conscience if I did." The grandmother also argues that since the children have already been to Florida, a trip to east Tennessee would be a broadening experience. One of the two older children, John Wesley (an eight-year-old boy), suggests that the grandmother does not have to join them. The little girl, June Star, chimes in that the grandmother would never let them go without her.

"The next morning the grandmother was the first one in the car, ready to go," O'Connor writes. Positioning herself in the middle of the back seat between John Wesley and June Star, she places a large black valise in the corner, concealing beneath it a basket containing her cat, Pitty Sing. O'Connor gives a detailed description of the grandmother's outfit, ending it with a foreshadowing remark: "In case of an accident, anyone seeing her dead on the highway would know at once that she was a lady." After traveling outside their hometown of Atlanta, the family stops at The Tower for sandwiches. Inside the restaurant, its owner, Red Sammy Butts, relates a story about two guys who recently stole gas from his store. His wife says that you can't trust anyone today, which gives the grandmother an opportunity to bring The Misfit into the conversation. The ensuing conversation prompts Red Sammy to make the title's claim: "A good man is hard to find." "He and the grandmother discussed better times," O'Connor tells us. After they theorize about the cause of society's decline, the family leaves The Tower and gets back on the road.

From this point on, the story literally turns off the main road after the grandmother suggests that they visit an old plantation, which she had visited years ago as a young lady. In an effort to convince her son to take the family on this side excursion, she fibs about secret panels and hidden family silver in order to excite John Wesley and June Star into pleading with Bailey. Eventually the grandmother and the children win out: Bailey turns the car around and heads for the dirt road leading to the plantation. His warning to everybody that this will be their only stop is darkly ironic.

As the family drives toward the plantation, the grandmother realizes that the house she is looking for is not actually in Georgia; its true location is in Tennessee. Her shock and embarrassment at this realization causes her to accidentally kick the valise, startling the cat out of the basket and onto Bailey's shoulder. Bailey loses control of the car. The children are hurled to the floor; the mother, holding the baby, is thrown out the door and onto the ground; the grandmother is flung into the front seat. Bailey, with the cat still clinging to his neck, remains frozen in the driver's seat.

The children waste little time worrying about injuries, so great is their delight at being in a genuine accident. Meanwhile, the mother sits in a ditch with the screaming baby and a broken shoulder, and the grandmother lays huddled beneath the dashboard, praying for an injury, which might soften Bailey's anger toward her.

As the grandmother hobbles out of the car, June Star expresses disappointment that no one has been killed. "The grandmother decided that she would not mention that the house was in Tennessee," O'Connor says dryly. A few minutes after the accident, with all of the shaken adults huddled in the ditch, the family notices a "a hearse-like automobile" approaching slowly from the top of a hill. The grandmother takes the initiative and waves the car down. The car stops just above them and three men, each carrying a gun, walk toward them. The grandmother recognizes the leader and declares excitedly, "You're The Misfit!" The man smiles and responds in his back-country dialect—a staple in virtually all of O'Connor's fiction—that "it would have been better for all of you, lady, if you hadn't of reckernized me."

O'Connor has created a back-country southern setting, in which a unique set of circumstances has led a family into a situation where the sacred and the profane will appear to be oddly intertwined. Evil appears to have intensely theological significance.

As the impending danger becomes palpable and the family's fear soars, the grandmother starts appealing to the goodness of The Misfit, engaging him in what O'Connor brilliantly portrays as a relatively casual (from The Misfit's perspective), but deeply philosophical and theological conversation. As they converse, The Misfit calmly sends members of the family into the nearby woods with his henchmen to be shot to death. With each shooting, the grandmother becomes more deliriously and desperately religious, while The Misfit remains relatively composed and grows increasingly reflective. He explains that he calls himself The Misfit "because I can't make what all I done wrong fit what all I gone through in punishment." He claims that Jesus was wrong to raise the dead and that there exists "no pleasure but meanness." The rest of her family has been killed at this point, and the grandmother falls into a state of complete delirium. She reaches out to The Misfit one last time. "Why you're one of my babies," she tells him. "You're one of my own children!"

When she touches him on the shoulder, The Misfit recoils and shoots her three times in the chest. After giving the order to throw the grandmother's body away with the others, he says sarcastically to Bobby Lee, one of the gunmen, "She would of been a good woman if it had been somebody there to shoot her every minute of her life." O'Connor ends the story two lines later, with The Misfit repeating his earlier statement: "It's no real pleasure in life." ❀

List of Characters in
"A Good Man Is Hard to Find"

The grandmother is the central character in this story and the first one O'Connor introduces. She tries to alter the family's plans to travel to Florida, but her wishes are disregarded. On the morning of the family's departure, she hides her cat in a basket in the car. After the family stops for sandwiches, she manages to convince her son, Bailey, to venture off the main road to see an old plantation house that she had visited as a girl. When she realizes that the house is actually in another state, she accidentally upsets the basket containing her cat, which springs onto Bailey's shoulder, causing him to have a car accident. When The Misfit arrives, it is the grandmother who identifies him, thereby ensuring the family's doom.

Bailey is the grandmother's son and the driver of the family car. Bailey consistently displays annoyance with his mother until just before his death. He becomes noticeably agitated at the grandmother's request to go off the main road, but he relents after being hounded by her and his two older children. After the accident, he heaves his mother's cat into a tree and seems to enter a silent rage. He and his son, John Wesley, are the first ones taken to the woods and shot to death.

The Misfit is first mentioned in the story's opening paragraph, when the grandmother waves a newspaper article about the outlaw in her son's face. The article describes The Misfit as an escaped felon believed to be headed for Florida. He appears to the family in person after the accident, with his two flunkies, and orders them to shoot the family members. He shoots the grandmother himself, however.

June Star and *John Wesley* are the antagonistic children who ride in the back seat with their grandmother. It is because of their relentless nagging that Bailey agrees to change course from the main road. Both children become extremely excited when they realize that they have been in a genuine accident.

The mother and *the baby* are essentially silent throughout the story. The mother makes no attempt to discipline her two older children, who are not very mannerly. The mother is injured in the car accident and is ultimately shot to death with the rest of the family.

Red Sammy Butts and *his wife* own The Tower, where the family stops for sandwiches before they stray from the main road.

Bobby Lee and *Hiram* are The Misfit's henchmen. They follow Misfit's orders to shoot each family member—except for the grandmother—in the woods. ❁

Critical Views on
"A Good Man Is Hard to Find"

HAROLD C. GARDINER, S. J., ON O'CONNOR'S CLARITY
OF VISION

[Harold C. Gardiner, S. J. (1904–1969), was a Roman
Catholic clergyman and the staff editor for the *New
Catholic Encyclopedia*. His publications include *Mysteries
End* (1946) and *Movies, Morals and Art* (1961). In this
essay, Gardiner discusses O'Connor's clear depiction of sin
and evil in her stories.]

It is generally the sentimental who are shocked by the grotesque, and in
Flannery O'Connor's artistic makeup there is not the slightest trace of
sentimentality. Her pity is not sentimental, because it springs from the
double view pointed out by Father Vann: it sees clearly the "nature of
sin itself," and the "immaturity of evil in the human heart." The most
obvious incarnation of evil in all her work is probably The Misfit in "A
Good Man Is Hard to Find." His cold-eyed wanton butchery of the
grandmother and the five others is the act of one apparently hardened
in crime; it is a heinous sin. But yet—but yet, who are we to judge, Miss
O'Connor seems to say. What forces have warped these minds so that
they come almost as it were to play with murder? Are they mature
humans? Is their grotesquerie only ours writ large?

> "Turn to the right, it was a wall," The Misfit said, looking up again at
> the cloudless sky. "Turn to the left, it was a wall. Look up it was a
> ceiling, look down it was a floor. I forget what I done, lady. I set there
> and set there, trying to remember what it was I done and I ain't
> recalled it to this day. Oncet in a while, I would think it was coming
> to me, but it never come."

When the old grandmother, sensing her impending murder, begins
to cry upon Jesus:

> "Yes'm," The Misfit said as if he agreed. "Jesus thrown everything off
> balance. It was the same case with Him as with me except He hadn't
> committed any crime and they could prove I had committed one
> because they had the papers on me . . . I call myself The Misfit . . .
> because I can't make what all I done wrong fit what all I gone
> through in punishment."

And as the murders continue down in the woods, The Misfit concludes:

> "Jesus was the only One that ever raised the dead . . . and He shouldn't have done it. He thown everything off balance. If he did what He said, then it's nothing for you to do but thow away everything and follow Him, and if He didn't, then it's nothing for you to do but to enjoy the few minutes you got left the best way you can—by killing somebody or burning down his house or doing some other meanness to him. No pleasure but meanness," he said and his voice had become almost a snarl.

> —Harold C. Gardiner, S. J., "Flannery O'Connor's Clarity of Vision." In *The Added Dimension: The Art and Mind of Flannery O'Connor,* eds. Melvin J. Friedman and Lewis A. Lawson (New York: Fordham University Press, 1966), pp. 190–191

IRVING MALIN ON O'CONNOR AND THE GROTESQUE

[Irving Malin (b. 1934) became a full professor at the City University of New York in 1972. His publications include *Critical Views of Isaac Bashevis Singer* (1969) and *The Achievement of Carson McCullers* (1982). In this essay, Malin focuses on the elements of the grotesque in O'Connor's fiction.]

The stories in *A Good Man Is Hard to Find* are set in the same unbalanced world of *Wise Blood*. The villains are "flat" narcissists who love themselves more than Jesus. Their displacement is again represented by dominating images of entrapment, "falling," and odd vision. I can explore closely only three stories: "A Good Man Is Hard to Find," "The Artificial Nigger," and "The Displaced Person."

In "A Good Man Is Hard to Find" The Misfit is the same kind of fanatic as Hazel Motes. He also believes that things would be different if Jesus had really done what He said:

> [He] thown everything off balance. If He did what He said, then it's nothing for you to do but thow away everything and follow Him, and if He didn't, then it's nothing for you to do but enjoy the few minutes you got left the best way you can—by killing somebody or burning down his house or doing some other meanness to him. No pleasure but meanness.

Although The Misfit claims that everything is Jesus' fault—if He ever lived!—he does not plan to let things stand. He will right the balance. *He will be the new Jesus of self-love.* But his Church of meanness gives him no pleasure or salvation. He continues to be anxious, empty, and metallic.

Miss O'Connor introduces a foil to The Misfit: the grandmother is a good person on the surface—at least the community thinks so—but she is also "mean." She forces her family to obey her; she sees them as an extension of herself; and she seizes "every chance to change" reality. Because she convinces her son to turn the car toward the house with the "secret panel," causing the family to meet The Misfit, she seals everyone's death. She tries to adopt The Misfit, giving him well-meaning advice and false love. He responds by shooting her three times.

Throughout the story Miss O'Connor uses images to reinforce the horror of self-love. The Tower, a restaurant owned by Red Sammy, is a "broken-down place"—"a long dark room" with tables, counter, and little dancing space. Once people went here to find pleasure; now Red Sammy is afraid to leave the door unlatched: he has succumbed to the "meanness" of the world. The plantation house which the Grandmother remembers is apparently peaceful—a sanctuary contrasted to the hellish Tower—and it holds glorious treasure. But Miss O'Connor shows us that this house—does it even exist?—is never reached; indeed, the Grandmother's self-centered wish to see it causes The Misfit to discover and murder the family. But houses are, in effect, wrecks of the spirit.

—Irving Malin, "Flannery O'Connor and the Grotesque." In *The Added Dimension: The Art and Mind of Flannery O'Connor*, eds. Melvin J. Friedman and Lewis A. Lawson (New York: Fordham University Press, 1966), pp. 113–114

FREDERICK J. HOFFMAN ON THE SEARCH FOR REDEMPTION IN O'CONNOR'S FICTION

[Frederick J. Hoffman (1909–1967), was a distinguished professor of English at the University of Wisconsin until his death in 1967. His publications include *The Achievement of D. H. Lawrence* (1953), *The Great Gatsby: A Study* (1962), and *The Art of Southern Fiction: A Study of Some Modern Novelists* (1967). This essay deals with the search for redemption in O'Connor's fiction.]

Miss O'Connor writes about intensely religious acts and dilemmas in a time when people are much divided on the question of what actually determines a "religious act." Definitions are not easy, and, frequently, what is being done with the utmost seriousness seems terribly naive, or simple-minded, to the reader. She must, therefore, force the statement of it into a pattern of "grotesque" action, which reminds one somewhat of Franz Kafka, at least in its violation of normal expectations.

We have the phenomenon of a Catholic writer describing a Protestant, an evangelical, world, to a group of readers who need to be forced or shocked and/or amused into accepting the validity of religious states. The spirit of evil abounds, and the premonition of disaster is almost invariably confirmed. Partly, this is because the scene is itself grotesquely exaggerated (though eminently plausible at the same time); partly it is because Christian sensibilities have been, not so much blunted as rendered bland and over-simple. The contrast of the fumbling grandmother and The Misfit in Miss O'Connor's most famous story, "A Good Man Is Hard to Find," is a case in point. The grandmother is fully aware of the expected terror, but she cannot react "violently" to it. She must therefore use commonplaces to meet a most uncommon situation:

> "If you would pray," the old lady said, "Jesus would help you."
> "That's right," The Misfit said.
> "Well then, why don't you pray?" she asked trembling with delight suddenly.
> "I don't want no hep," he said.
> "I'm doing all right by myself."

Another truth about Miss O'Connor's fiction is its preoccupation with the Christ figure, a use of Him that is scarcely equalled by her contemporaries. The Misfit offers an apparently strange but actually a not uncommon observation:

> "Jesus was the only One that ever raised the dead, . . . and He shouldn't have done it. He thown everything off balance. If He did

what He said, then it's nothing for you to do but thow away everything and follow Him, and if He didn't, then it's nothing for you to
do but enjoy the few minutes you got left the best you can—by killing
somebody or burning down his house or doing some other meanness
to him. No pleasure but meanness," he said and his voice became
almost a snarl.

—Frederick J. Hoffman, "The Search for Redemption." In *The Added
Dimension: The Art and Mind of Flannery O'Connor*, eds. Melvin J.
Friedman and Lewis A. Lawson (New York: Fordham University
Press, 1966), pp. 33–34

CLAIRE KAHANE ON FLANNERY O'CONNOR'S RANGE OF VISION

[Claire Kahane (b. 1935) is a professor of English at the
State University of New York at Buffalo. She coedited *In
Dora's Case: Freud Hysteria, Feminism* (1985) and also pub-
lished *Passions of the Voice: Hysteria, Narrative and the
Figure of the Speaking Woman* (1995). In this essay, Kahane
discusses the details which enhance the grotesque in
O'Connor's fiction.]

Traditionally, it is this admixture of the uncanny and the comic
which comprises the grotesque. While "grotesque" has been the word
used to label O'Connor's world, it has not been used to explain it. In
his essay "The Uncanny," Freud has provided a key to understanding
the essential aspect of the grotesque. The uncanny exists "when
repressed infantile complexes have been revived by some impression,
or when the primitive beliefs we have surmounted seem once more
to be confirmed." As elements which compose the uncanny, he lists
the castration complex, womb fantasies, the idea of the double, the
animistic conception of the universe, the omnipotence of thoughts,
and the primitive fear of the dead—all concepts of very early mental
life which, when they emerge in the context of ordinary adult reality,
have the effect of weakening our ego faculty. These elements, skill-
fully integrated into the imagery of O'Connor's fiction, are responsible for its disturbingly grotesque quality.

Even when an image is not itself objectively threatening, O'Connor can make it so by a vividness of inconsequential detail which in its special intensity suggests a deflection of focus from something frightening to something reassuringly innocuous. For example, in *Wise Blood*, O'Connor's seemingly gratuitous description of the ash on a cigarette about an inch long creates the impression of displaced attention, and thus contributes to the sense of apprehension in the novel. An instant before Guizac is crushed by a tractor in "The Displaced Person," Mrs. McIntyre sees "his feet and legs and trunk sticking imprudently out from the side of the tractor. He had on rubber boots that were cracked and splashed with mud. He raised one knee and then lowered it and turned himself slightly." Perhaps the most brilliant use of this prolonged focus on inconsequential detail is the succession of irrelevant description ending with an almost parenthetical but climactic image in this passage from "A Good Man Is Hard to Find":

> [The car] came to a stop just over them and for some minutes, the driver looked down with a steady expressionless gaze to where they were sitting, and didn't speak. Then he turned his head and muttered something to the other two and they got out. One was a fat boy in black trousers and a red sweat shirt with a silver stallion embossed on the front of it. . . . The other had on khaki pants and a blue striped coat and a gray hat pulled down very low, hiding most of his face. . . .
>
> The driver got out of the car and stood by the side of it, looking down at them. He was an older man than the other two. His hair was just beginning to gray and he wore silver-rimmed spectacles that gave him a scholarly look. He had a long creased face and didn't have on any shirt or undershirt. He had on blue jeans that were too tight for him and was holding a black hat and a gun. The two boys *also had guns.* (italics mine)

In extremely frightening experiences, psychoanalyst Phyllis Greenacre notes, "inconsequential details of the scene . . . stick in the mind as inexplicably vivid, although the central horror of the experience is not missing." With the psychological acumen of the artist, O'Connor characteristically focuses on such details to intensify horror.

—Claire Kahane, "Flannery O'Connor's Range of Vision." In *Critical Essays on Flannery O'Connor*, eds. Melvin J. Friedman and Beverly Lyon Clark (Boston: G. K. Hall & Co., 1985), pp. 123–124

[Ruthann Knechel Johansen is Assistant Director of the
Interdisciplinary Core Course at the University of Notre
Dame. She was the recipient of the 1992 Elizabeth Agee
Prize in American Literature. Her book, *The Narrative
Secret of Flannery O'Connor,* was published in 1994. In this
chapter, Johansen focuses on the element of sin in
O'Connor's stories.]

From the opening conversations in "A Good Man Is Hard to Find"
taking place among the family members preparing for their Florida
trip until the grandmother is shot, the characters bombard each
other with words that never carry a message across the space
between characters but ricochet off each other, leaving each person
alone. The grandmother who rails against a trip to Florida tries to
influence the family plans through fear of an escaped convict. Her
state of alarm ("Yes and what would you do if this fellow, The Misfit,
caught you?") is met by flippant retort from her young grandson
("I'd smack his face") and by an appraisal of her grandmother's
character from June Star ("She wouldn't stay home for a million
bucks. Afraid she'd miss something. She has to go everywhere we
go"). Apparently forgetting the intention of her original comment,
or else effectively sidetracked by the verbal barrage that hasn't
acknowledged her real interests, the grandmother now retaliates,
"Just remember that the next time you want me to curl your hair."

This same process of deflection occurs when the grandmother and
The Misfit sit on the ground talking. After assuring him that he's a
good man, "not a bit common," the grandmother listens to The
Misfit tell her his daddy's appraisal of him—"it's some that can live
their whole life out without asking about it and it's others has to
know why it is, and this boy is one of the latters." In the midst of this
self-disclosure The Misfit interrupts himself to demonstrate a
bizarre concern for social convention: "I'm sorry I don't have a shirt
on before you ladies. . . .We buried our clothes that we had on when
we escaped and we're just making do until we can get better. We borrowed these from some folks we met." And though following the literal meaning of the words and being herself concerned with social
approbation but ignorant of both the criminal and religious impli-

cations of wearing borrowed clothes, the grandmother responds, "That's perfectly all right . . . maybe Bailey has an extra shirt in his suitcase."

Into a maximally alarming situation O'Connor has inserted exchanges of words that disclose family history, defer to social manners, and remind us that The Misfit, reminiscent of Job who could not make his crime match his punishment, asks hard questions of life and identifies himself with Jesus: "Jesus thown everything off balance. It was the same case with him as with me except He hadn't committed any crime and they could prove I had committed one because they had the papers on me. . . . I call myself The Misfit . . . because I can't make what all I done wrong fit what all I gone through in punishment." A scream from the woods interrupts The Misfit's flow of words, but he resumes undisturbed, "Does it seem right to you, lady, that one is punished a heap and another ain't punished at all?" Yet as such philosophizing occurs, recalling age-old debates about theodicy, the murders proceed without question.

—Ruthann Knechel Johansen, *The Narrative Secret of Flannery O'Connor* (Tuscaloosa, AL: The University of Alabama Press, 1994), pp. 37–38

ROBERT H. BRINKMEYER, JR. ON ASCETICISM AND THE IMAGINATIVE VISION OF O'CONNOR

[Robert H. Brinkmeyer, Jr. is professor of American Literature and Southern Studies at the University of Mississippi. His publications include *Three Catholic Writers of the Modern South* (1985) and *Katherine Anne Porter's Artistic Development: Primitivism, Traditionalism, and Totalitarianism*. In this essay, Brinkmeyer discusses the vision in O'Connor's approach.]

Dead is precisely the condition in which a number of O'Connor's characters end up, most of them having been shocked out of their complacent everyday existence by some act of intense violence that propels them to a complete acceptance of Christ—an acceptance so overwhelming and pure that their spiritual houses are indeed in order, freed from any taint of doubt or unrest. As Frederick Asals has persuasively argued, this motion toward a totally unquestioning faith involves the "purification of the rebellious self," "a cleansing of [the character's] most cherished illusions, or indeed of any loving self at all." Asals rightly terms this motion of stripping away of the prideful self ascetic, and he argues that the intense pressure of this ascetic motion toward radical acts of self-denial drives O'Connor's fiction forward and best embodies the essential cast of her imagination. Asals locates the primary source of O'Connor's asceticism in the predominant religion of her homeland, southern fundamentalism, a faith that demands that its believers make the uncompromising choice of either accepting Christ (and thereby giving up the world to follow Him) or of denying Him (and thereby choosing the world and its sinfulness). The Misfit in "A Good Man Is Hard to Find" knows the fundamentalist imperative, saying of Christ and the choice that everyone must make in regard to Him: "If He did what He said, then it's nothing for you to do but throw away everything and follow Him, and if He didn't, then it's nothing for you to do but enjoy the few minutes you got left the best way you can—by killing somebody or burning down his house or doing some other meanness to him. No pleasure but meanness." In her deep sympathies with such thinking, O'Connor, says Asals, creates a deeply ascetic fiction in which the emphasis is "not on a bringing together, but on a splitting apart, not on harmony, but on sundering."

There is no doubt that O'Connor deeply identified with southern fundamentalists. In her letters and essays, she frequently speaks of her admiration for and affinities with fundamentalist fanatics, particularly their intense and rigorous brand of faith. In "The Catholic Novelist in the Protestant South," she suggests that her "underground religious affinities" lie with "backwoods prophets and shouting fundamentalists" and that these feelings are shaping forces in her imaginative life. She says that when the southern Catholic writer descends within himself to find himself and his region (the pronouns are hers, and she includes herself in the discussion), he discovers there "a feeling of kinship [with the fundamentalists] strong enough to spur him to write."

—Robert H. Brinkmeyer, Jr., "Asceticism and the Imaginative Vision of Flannery O'Connor." In *Flannery O'Connor: New Perspectives,* eds. Sura P. Rath and Mary Neff Shaw (Athens, GA: The University of Georgia Press, 1996), pp. 178–179

Plot Summary of
"Good Country People"

"Good Country People," the final and only previously unpublished story to appear in O'Connor's first collection of stories *A Good Man Is Hard to Find*, opens with a description of the three basic facial expressions worn by Mrs. Freeman, the hired hand on the Hopewell farm. O'Connor describes Mrs. Freeman's morning routine of dropping in to gossip with Mrs. Hopewell, while Joy sullenly endures their discourse on "important issues." Two frequent topics are Mrs. Freeman's teenage daughters, Glynese and Carramae. Neither daughter appears in the story, but O'Connor tells us through Mrs. Freeman that 18-year-old Glynese is sought after by many eligible men, while 15-year-old Carramae is married, pregnant, and constantly vomiting. Mrs. Hopewell is the long-divorced mother of 32-year-old Joy, "a large blonde girl who had an artificial leg." Despite Mrs. Freeman's nosy nature, Mrs. Hopewell is satisfied with the farming services of Mrs. Freeman and her husband, and she considers them to be "good country people." This characterization recurs throughout the story to describe various characters, whose "good country" nature comes under the author's scrutiny.

At the beginning of the story, O'Connor describes in detail the various idiosyncrasies of Mrs. Freeman, Mrs. Hopewell, and Joy. We discover some four pages into the story that when Joy was 21 years old, she legally changed her name to Hulga, because of its distinctly unpleasant sound and the effect that the name would have on her mother. "She saw it as the name of her highest creative act," O'Connor writes. "One of her major triumphs was that her mother had not been able to turn her dust into Joy, but the greater one was that she had been able to turn it herself into Hulga." Joy-Hulga's efforts to perturb her mother with the new name are effective. Although Mrs. Hopewell prides herself on her tolerance and is fond of expressions such as, "It takes all kinds to make the world," O'Connor makes it clear that Mrs. Hopewell is utterly baffled by and disappointed in her graceless, abrasive bookworm of a daughter.

As the story proceeds, we learn that Joy-Hulga holds a Ph.D. in philosophy and is not only filled with resentment toward her mother, but also feels intellectually superior to her. In fact, Joy-Hulga feels that everyone else is incapable of understanding her genius. We also discover that in addition to her missing leg (which was shot off by her father in a hunting accident when Joy was 10 years old), Hulga has a weak heart and is not expected to live past the age of 45. Although she pities her daughter, Mrs. Hopewell is unnerved by Hulga's intellectual pursuits and would feel uncomfortable telling others that her daughter is a philosopher.

It is just after O'Connor has established these characters as three distinctly different people who happen to be equally shallow and spiritually vacant that she introduces a new character: Manley Pointer is a lanky, 19-year-old Bible salesperson who claims to have a heart condition. Although the story begins the morning after his visit, the author employs a flashback to recount his stay at the Hopewell's farm the previous night.

Manley appeared at the Hopewell's door carrying a large black suitcase full of Bibles and displaying an earnest, unsophisticated disposition. In a seemingly innocent manner, he maneuvered his way inside and declared himself a genuine country boy, prompting Mrs. Hopewell to state that "good country people are the salt of the earth." Manley went on to claim that because he had a heart condition, he was devoting his life to "Chrustian service." His supposed "heart condition" struck a sentimental chord with Mrs. Hopewell, because of Joy's genuine heart problem. She invited him to dinner, after which he left the Hopewells—but not before speaking privately with Hulga outside and arranging to meet her for a picnic lunch the following day.

O'Connor then returns us to the present, as Mrs. Freedman chatters to Mrs. Hopewell, who is wondering what her daughter said to Manley the previous night. When Hulga senses that her secret exchange with Manley Pointer is about to become a topic of breakfast conversation, she "stumps" off to her room and locks the door. O'Connor then leads her readers inside Hulga's mind, exposing her self-righteous rationale for consenting to meet with Manley Pointer. She had dreamt the previous night that she would seduce Manley and then enlighten him to the intricacies of her moral and theological philosophy, reassuring herself that "true genius can get an idea across even to an inferior mind."

Hulga heads for the arranged meeting place at exactly ten o'clock in the morning, managing to flee from her house undetected.

Manley emerges from behind the bushes with his briefcase in hand and they proceed to walk into the woods. After some awkward exchanges about the Bible and Hulga's wooden leg, Hulga declares that she doesn't believe in God. Manley acts surprised, then plants a heavy kiss upon her lips. This begins what O'Connor masterfully portrays as a verbal contest for control, with each character maneuvering from what appears to be opposite sides of the spiritual spectrum.

After a series of statements about religion and damnation, Manley cleverly tricks Hulga into climbing up into the loft of a barn. Once they are both lying in the straw, Manley begins kissing Hulga, removing (and pocketing) her glasses in the process. She counters Manley's kisses and declarations of love with an intellectual shield, which Manley breaks down by tenderly asking to see where her artificial leg attaches to her stump.

She surrenders completely to what she sees as Manley's pure innocence and allows him to remove her leg. Before the narrative lapses into sentimentality, we are brilliantly redirected by O'Connor into a stark turn to the grotesque.

Pushing Hulga's leg out of reach, Manley pulls a flask of whiskey from a hollowed-out Bible, spreads a pack of pornographic playing cards out before her, and hands her a box of condoms. Barely capable of speech, Hulga manages to mutter, "Aren't you just good country people?" Manley replies, "Yeah, but it ain't held me back none."

The loft scene culminates in Hulga's strikingly ironic claim that Manley is a "perfect Christian" in his hypocrisy, leading him to retort that he is not so simple as to "believe in that crap." He then proceeds to gather his possessions—and Hulga's wooden leg—all the while bragging that he will never be caught because he robs people under a new alias wherever he goes. He leaves her helpless in the loft with his final parting shot: "you ain't so smart. I been believing in nothing ever since I was born!"

The story ends much as it began, looking out from the perspective of Mrs. Freeman and Mrs. Hopewell. They are working together in the back pasture of the Hopewell farm when they see Manley emerge from the woods and head out toward the road. "He was so simple, but I guess the world would be better off if we were all that simple," says Mrs. Hopewell with unwitting irony. "Some can't be that simple," Mrs. Freeman replies. "I know I never could." ❀

List of Characters in
"Good Country People"

Mrs. Freeman is the wife of Mrs. Hopewell's tenant farmer. She is the first character the reader encounters. Mrs. Hopewell considers her a nosy, "good country" person. She and her husband, who plays no part in the story, have been working for the Hopewells for four years. She is a fixture in the Hopewell house and is very much a part of their daily affairs. She delivers the final line in the story.

Mrs. Hopewell, the divorced owner of the farm, is the mother of Joy-Hulga. She is fond of using a handful of cliched statements that make her appear tolerant of other people. She is the first to meet Manley Pointer, the Bible salesman, and she invites him to stay for dinner. She and Mrs. Freeman begin and end the story in gossipy conversation.

Joy/Hulga Hopewell is the 32-year-old daughter of Mrs. Hopewell. She has a Ph.D. in philosophy, but lives at home because of a weak heart. Her leg was shot off at age 10, and she "stumps" around on her wooden leg. She accompanies Manley Pointer, the young Bible salesman, into the woods, intending to seduce him sexually and intellectually. She becomes his victim in the end, when Manley leaves her stranded in the hayloft of a barn without her leg or her glasses.

Manley Pointer is the scrawny, 19-year-old Bible salesman who turns out to be a con artist. He appears at the Hopewell home to sell his Bibles, but works the visit into an invitation to dinner. The following day, he escorts Joy/Hulga into the woods, where he lures her into the hayloft of a barn and then makes off with her artificial leg and her glasses. ❀

Critical Views on
"Good Country People"

ROBERT DRAKE ON O'CONNOR'S FICTION

[Robert Drake (b. 1930) became a professor of English at the University of Tennessee, Knoxville in 1973. His publications include *Amazing Grace* (1965) and *The Single Heart* (1971). In this essay, Drake focuses on the idiosyncrasies of O'Connor's characters.]

Another shocker among these stories is "Good Country People." Here Joy Hopewell (who has changed her name to Hulga, perhaps to spite her genteel mother), with a Ph.D. in philosophy and a wooden leg which she is as sensitive about as a peacock is his tail, almost as though it were her soul really, is duped by a "Christian" Bible salesman whom she had thought to seduce by way of assault on his Christianity—and perhaps his masculinity. But the Bible salesman wins hands down: he says he doesn't believe in Christianity. ("I may sell Bibles but I know which end is up and I wasn't born yesterday and I know where I'm going.") Furthermore, using the name Hulga (which she regards as "her highest creative act") "as if he didn't think much of it," he concludes, "You ain't so smart. I been believing in nothing ever since I was born!" And he walks off with her wooden leg, which has fascinated him as the thing which makes her "different." Again, it's the sort of Anti-Christ figure of the Bible salesman who wins something of our admiration: he may be a devil but he's not, as is Hulga, a fool (and an "educated" one at that).

The mother, Mrs. Hopewell (the name seems too symbolic to gloss over, and Miss O'Connor *is* almost openly allegorical at times), is one of her familiar genteel women. She is a "good Christian woman," perhaps like Mrs. May in "Greenleaf" in the posthumous volume who thinks "the word, Jesus, should be kept inside the church building like other words inside the bedroom. She was a good Christian woman with a large respect for religion, though she did not, of course, believe any of it was true." Perhaps also Mrs. Hopewell has something in common with old Mrs. Crater of "The Life You Save May Be Your Own," who, when reminded by the sanctimonious con man, Mr. Shiftlet, that the monks of old slept in their coffins, replies, very smugly, "They wasn't as advanced as we are." (Mrs. Hopewell *is* irked that Hulga is a student of philosophy. "That was something that had ended with the Greeks and Romans.") But Miss O'Connor takes a dim view of modern man's "advancement": again and again, she demonstrates a profound distrust in "progress" and "enlightenment" which are won at the expense of the sacramental, whole view of life. And one feels that Tarwater, the teenage prophet of *The Violent Bear It Away*, may be speaking for her when he scorns flying as just another form of justification by technology: "I wouldn't give you nothing for no airplane. A buzzard can fly."

—Robert Drake, *Flannery O'Connor: A Critical Essay* (William B. Eerdmans Publishing Co., 1966), pp. 24–26

C. HUGH HOLMAN ON O'CONNOR AND THE SOUTHERN LITERARY TRADITION

[C. Hugh Holman (1914–1981) was a professor of English at the University of North Carolina, Chapel Hill, until his death in 1981. His publications include *Another Man's Poison* (1947), *The Loneliness at the Core: Studies in Thomas Wolfe* (1975), and *Windows on the World: Essays on American Social Fiction* (1979). In this essay, Holman discusses O'Connor's connection to the Southern literary tradition.]

She is more nearly central to the Southern literary tradition in her persistent passion for order. Confronted with a modern, mechanized, scientifically-oriented world, the leading literary spokesmen for the South have usually shared the discomfort that most producers of humane art experience in the presence of the mechanical, and, like the twelve at Vanderbilt in 1930, they "tend to support a Southern way of life against what may be called the American or prevailing way." Almost all artists feel a hunger for meaning, a need for structure, and rage for order in existence, and believe that the human spirit should never calmly surrender its endless search for order. Twentieth-century writers confronted by the spectacle of the mechanized culture of America have taken many different roads to many different regions of the spirit. Some have sought in art itself a kind of solipsistic answer to the need of order and thus have made a religion of art. Some have sought in activist movements bent on social change a way to establish meaning in the world. The Southerner, predisposed to look backward as a result of his concern with the past, has tended to impose a desire for a social structure that reflects moral principles and he has tried to see in the past of his region at least the shadowy outlines of a viable and admirable moral-social world. Allen Tate, in 1952, in a retrospective glance at the Agrarian movement said:

> I never thought of Agrarianism as a *restoration* of anything in the Old South; I saw it as something to be created, as I think it will in the long run be created as the result of a profound change, not only in the South, but elsewhere, in the moral and religious outlook of western man. . . . What I had in mind twenty years ago . . . presupposes, with us, a prior order, the order of a unified Christendom. The Old South perpetuated many of the virtues of such an order; but to try to "revive" the Old South, and to build a wall around it, would be a kind of idolatry; it would prefer the accident to the substance. If there is a useful program that we might undertake in the South, would it not be towards the greater unity of the varieties of Southern Protestantism, with the ultimate aim the full unity of all Christians? We are told by our Northern friends that the greatest menace to the South is ignorance; but there is even greater ignorance of the delusion of progressive enlightenment.

Miss O'Connor was generally in sympathy with such views of the Agrarians. When she makes statements such as this one from "The Fiction Writer and His Country" she seems almost to be echoing their beliefs: "The anguish that most of us have observed for some time now has been caused not by the fact that the South is alienated from the rest of the country, but by the fact that it is not alienated enough, that every day we are getting more and more like the rest of the country, that we are being forced out, not only of our many sins but of our few virtues." And certainly one could hardly call a friend of science the creator of Hulga Hopewell, in "Good Country People," who has a Ph.D. in philosophy, a wooden leg, and a willingness to be seduced by a fake Bible salesman who steals the leg and leaves her betrayed and helpless in the hay loft. Hulga underlines this statement in one of the books that she endlessly reads and marks up:

Science, on the other hand, has to assert its soberness and seriousness afresh and declare that it is concerned solely with what-is. Nothing—how can it be for science anything but a horror and a phantasm? If science is right, then one thing stands firm: science wishes to know nothing of nothing. Such is after all the strictly scientific approach to Nothing. We know it by wishing to know nothing of Nothing.

—C. Hugh Holman, "Her Rue with a Difference." In *The Added Dimension: The Art and Mind of Flannery O'Connor*, eds. Melvin J. Friedman and Lewis A. Lawson (New York: Fordham University Press, 1966), pp. 78-80

DOROTHY TUCK MCFARLAND ON O'CONNOR'S BOOK *A GOOD MAN IS HARD TO FIND*

[Dorothy Tuck McFarland (b. 1938), has worked as a teacher, an editor, and a critic. Her publications include *Crowell's Handbook of Faulkner* (1964) and *Willa Cather* (1972). In this excerpt from her book *Flannery O'Connor*, McFarland analyzes "Good Country People" in the context of the stories in O'Connor's collection *A Good Man Is Hard to Find*.]

"Good Country People," the penultimate story in the collection, is something of a comic variation on "A Good Man Is Hard to Find." As the grandmother of the title story thinks of herself as a good Christian woman who believes in all the conventional platitudes, Hulga Hopewell, the Ph.D. in philosophy who is the protagonist of "Good Country People," thinks of herself as a good nihilist who energetically disbelieves in all the conventional platitudes. In their titles both stories implicitly ask the reader to consider what are good men or good people. And in both stories O'Connor uses conventional language for comic and ironic purposes, emphasizing the meaninglessness of the platitudes in the mouths of her characters, and at the same time using their words to sound the main themes of the story. For instance, Hulga's mother, Mrs. Hopewell, characteristically strings together remarks like "Everybody is different. . . . It takes all kinds to make the world. . . . Nothing is perfect." Nevertheless, she actually tolerates differences and imperfections very poorly. Two of the themes in the story grow out of the characters' attitudes toward uniqueness ("everybody is different") and imperfection.

Mrs. Hopewell and her tenant's wife, Mrs. Freeman, embody contrasting ways of looking at the world that provide the frame for the story. Whereas Mrs. Hopewell is determined always to put a smiling face on things and never look beneath the surface, the gimlet-eyed Mrs. Freeman has a fondness for hidden things: "the details of secret infections, hidden deformities, assaults upon children." She is obsessed with the physical demands and ills of the body, and in her conversation about her two daughters she dwells on the details of two major aspects of their physical being: their sexuality and their ailments. One daughter, Glynese, is being courted by several admirers, one of whom is going to chiropractor school and who cures her of a sty by popping her neck. The other daughter, Carramae, is pregnant and unable to "keep anything on her stomach."

Mrs. Hopewell's daughter, Hulga, is antagonized by her mother's platitudinous optimism to the extent that her face has come to wear a look of constant outrage that "obliterated every other expression." She finds Mrs. Freeman tolerable only on the ground that Mrs. Freeman diverts some of her mother's attention from her; otherwise, she is uncomfortable with Mrs. Freeman's fascination with the secrets of the body.

—Dorothy Tuck McFarland, *Flannery O'Connor* (New York: Frederick Ungar Publishing Co., 1976), pp. 35–36

ANTHONY DI RENZO ON THE WORD, THE FLESH, AND THE GROTESQUE IN O'CONNOR'S FICTION

[Anthony Di Renzo (b. 1960) has been an assistant professor in the Writing Program at Ithaca College since 1991. He has published essays and stories in many literary journals and magazines such as *Tornado Alley* and *Kansas Review*. In this excerpt from his book, *American Gargoyles,* Di Renzo concentrates on the grotesque in O'Connor's fiction.]

The harsh laughter, grotesque hyperbole, and narrative detachment of "Good Country People" resemble that of the fabliau. Both observe the economy and dynamics of the joke or the tall tale. "Distance," says Norris Lacy, "is created not only by generic expectations and narrative economy; equally important is the artifice of subject matter or treatment. Despite the realistic descriptions of everyday life in the fabliaux, and despite the poet's frequent assertions of the truth of his stories, verisimilitude is not a principal concern." What is a principal concern is comic shock, in the sharpness of the story's punch line, the unexpectedness of its climactic reversal. Hulga's attempted seduction of the seemingly innocent Bible salesman, Manley Pointer, is the story's payoff, the moment when all of its sophisticated narrative elements come together only to be demolished by ribaldry and satire.

The hayloft scene in "Good Country People" is probably "one of the most bizarre representations" of romance in "our recent literature." It is a screamingly funny and disturbing portrayal of the delusions and manipulations of sexual seduction. Few passages in O'Connor are as explicit or contain as many double entendres. Manley Pointer is "certainly one of the most phallic names in fiction," and the scene itself is a variation on the familiar joke about the farmer's daughter and the traveling salesman. As Per Nykrog points out, the fabliau as a genre "burlesque"s the conventions of courtly romance. Hulga and Manley's tryst in the hayloft burlesques the conventions of American courtship. It is "stocked with the clichés of first love—hot breathing, sticky lips, awkward kisses, the requisite 'proof' of love." But these clichés take on a grotesque life of their own. Hulga rubs "Vapex" on her T-shirt as an aphrodisiac because she does not own "perfume." Manley carries condoms in a hollowed-out Bible: "THIS PRODUCT TO BE USED ONLY FOR THE PREVENTION OF DISEASE." A wooden leg becomes a token of virginity. Erotic fumbling has become monstrously funny, and the couple's love talk is no less bizarre or hilarious. Manley shyly initiates intimacy by asking Hulga, "You ever ate a chicken that was two days old?" Hulga's idea of tenderness is equally bathetic. "There mustn't be anything dishonest between us," she tells Manley, drawing him closer to her breast. "I am thirty years old . . . I have a number of degrees."

—Anthony Di Renzo, *American Gargoyles: Flannery O'Connor and the Medieval Grotesque* (Carbondale and Edwardsville: Southern Illinois University Press, 1993), pp. 74–75

[Jeanne Campbell Reesman is a professor of English at the
University of Texas in San Antonio and director of the divi-
sion of English, classics, and philosophy. Her publications
include *American Designs: The Late Novels of James and
Faulkner* (1991). In this essay, Reesman looks at how
O'Connor's language and her characterizations of women
contribute to the grotesque world she creates in "Good
Country People."]

The ocular metaphor in "Good Country People" is important, the
pattern coming to fruition when Joy/Hulga loses her eyeglasses at
the end of the story, but her internal vision has been readjusted. It is
in many ways a story about looking and not seeing, with great stress
laid on the repeated references to watching, eyes, or inner vision. But
from Joy/Hulga's squint to Glynese's sty, vision in this world is faulty,
perhaps the reason her father accidentally shot off her leg when she
was a child. Joy tells us that she sees from afar or "through to
nothing," but Manley's eyes are described as "steel spikes," and after
all he carries a glass eye he got from a previous conquest. Vision
itself is grotesque.

Opposed to reductive ocularity is a host of verbal images. Mrs.
Hopewell lies about having "the Word" in the house, and of course
Manley tries to make Joy/Hulga say she loves him. The cliché of the
title becomes terribly ironic; the literalizations of grotesque clichés
acknowledge truth, as Joy/Hulga hopes when she renames herself.
And when Manley, whose speech is the most countrified and awkward to start, asks Joy/Hulga whether she is shy, he dialogically
moves right to the point, so to speak. He reveals himself in language,
not appearance: when he says he believes in nothing we believe him.
At the end Joy/Hulga stumbles blindly with his final words aching in
her ears.

O'Connor's characters' self-hatred of the female body is sometimes overcome and sometimes not. Joy/Hulga's rage against her
femininity is grotesquely turned against itself, perhaps to heal her.
O'Connor holds out hope for those who are able to see and address
their grotesque selves; Joy/Hulga, "her face purple and her mouth
half full," earlier demands of her mother, when she can stand no

more of her and Mrs. Freeman's advice that "a smile never hurt anyone," "Woman! do you ever look inside? Do you ever look inside and see what you are *not?*'" Joy/Hulga has the opportunity to do just that, and in encountering her violation we not only witness her startling moment of self-knowledge, but also, through the story's grotesqueries, we find the boundaries blurred between our own world, inner and outer, verbal and visual. If Joy's "weak heart" is strengthened and her deformity overcome by a grotesque violation, we must continue to ask about the grotesque world in which this occurs, a world that goes on in Mrs. Freeman's and Mrs. Hopewell's inane conversation at the story's conclusion. How much of their conversation masks the violations of women that occur daily in their society? How much of what they say is a violation? O'Connor leaves us, like Joy/Hulga, waiting for answers.

—Jeanne Campbell Reesman, "Women, Language, and the Grotesque in Flannery O'Connor and Eudora Welty." In *Flannery O'Connor: New Perspectives*, eds. Sura P. Rath and Mary Neff Shaw (Athens, GA: The University of Georgia Press, 1996), pp. 46–47

JOANNE HALLERAN MCMULLEN ON STYLISTIC TECHNIQUES OF ANNIHILATION IN O'CONNOR'S FICTION

[Joanne Halleran McMullen's book *Writing against God: Language as Message in the Literature of Flannery O'Connor* was published in 1996 by the Mercer University Press. In this chapter, McMullen focuses on O'Connor's treatment of violence and death in her fiction.]

In addition to pronoun references and ambiguity, O'Connor continually deemphasizes the importance of individuals through naming techniques and an avoidance of names altogether. In "Good Country People," Joy herself changes the name her mother (and O'Connor) gave her. She, and O'Connor, decide on "Hulga" because as O'Connor writes:

> She had a vision of the name working like the ugly sweating Vulcan who stayed in the furnace and to whom, presumably, the goddess had to come when called. She saw it as the name of her highest creative act. One of her major triumphs was that her mother had not been able to turn her dust into Joy, but the greater one was that she had been able to turn it herself into Hulga.

As important as the creation of this name seems to be to both O'Connor and Joy, after Joy-Hulga decides to meet and seduce the Bible salesman, the name "Hulga" is only used twice. O'Connor has the Bible salesman refer to her by name when he first meets her for their "picnic." To her question of why he brought his Bibles, he answers, "You can never tell when you'll need the word of God, Hulga." And finally, at the end of the story when he has violated her spiritually, O'Connor has him say:

> "And I'll tell you another thing, Hulga," he said, using the name as if he didn't think much of it, "you ain't so smart. I been believing in nothing ever since I was born!" . . .

O'Connor's uses of "Hulga" at the beginning and end of this episode function as a framing device within which she establishes her main character's spiritual fate. She ironically has the Bible salesman signal that Hulga, the individual, might need the word of God, but for six pages Hulga's individuality is ignored. Not until she has been absolutely annihilated and left spiritually, emotionally, and physically devastated to consider her fate does O'Connor give her back her name. But this only for a moment, for O'Connor leaves Hulga with the sentence: "the girl was left sitting on the straw in the dusty sunlight." Perhaps O'Connor sees this image as presenting her readers with a newborn babe in the straw-filled manger ready after her trials to begin a new life in Christ. But the tension that develops between O'Connor's intended message and its overt form clashes here. By keeping her characters largely unspecified, and by focusing on ambiguous or neutral pronoun references or indefinite noun referents such as "the girl," O'Connor disengages herself from her characters, who are theologically important only as instruments through which God works. This stylistic technique seems to defeat her intense personal desire to deliver an audience antagonistic to a loving, caring, Catholic God into the religious society she feels they have rejected. Despite her detailed glosses, her language guides her readers away from her theological designs. The reader might rightly ask where is the linguistic message reinforcing the Christian directive "do unto others" or love of thy sister/brother, or that even the least of us is loved by God.

—Joanne Halleran McMullen, *Writing against God: Language as Message in the Literature of Flannery O'Connor* (Macon, GA: Mercer University Press, 1996), pp. 16–17

Plot Summary of
"Everything That Rises Must Converge"

"Everything That Rises Must Converge," the story that lends its title to Flannery O'Connor's posthumous collection, opens in the home of Julian and his mother. They are preparing to take a Wednesday evening bus ride to the downtown Y for a reducing class, since Julian's mother's doctor recommended that she lose weight. O'Connor tells the story in the third person, but from Julian's perspective. The central themes of the story emerge in its opening paragraph: the mother fears taking the buses alone at night "since they had been integrated." Julian resents feeling obligated to his mother, "but every Wednesday night, he braced himself and took her." We soon become aware that the emerging civil rights movement is a catalyst for Julian's antagonism toward his mother.

Before they leave to catch the bus, we learn that Julian's mother has spent what she fears is too much money on a flamboyant hat. Through the mother's misgivings about her purchase of the hat, O'Connor reveals the great emphasis that she places upon her appearance. We also learn that she comes from a once-prosperous and influential family as she tries to impress upon Julian the importance of "knowing who you are." The mother is clearly rooted in the traditions of the old South; Julian is swept up in the liberal ideals of the civil rights movement. O'Connor sees to it, however, that neither character is completely one-dimensional and therefore totally unworthy of sympathy.

On the walk to the bus stop, Julian's mother tries to encourage him about his future, telling him, "Rome wasn't built in a day." Julian—a would-be writer who is selling typewriters— remains "saturated in depression," and wishes for a selfish, drunken mother whom he could resent unconditionally. The conversation then turns to Julian's great-grandfather, a former governor who owned a plantation with 200 slaves. Julian and his mother view their ancestry in vastly different ways, although Julian's mother recalls that "there no better person in the world" than Caroline, the old black nurse who cared for her as a girl. In his irritation, Julian takes off his tie in hopes of getting a reaction from his mother. Julian's mother nags him until he puts it back on, all the while restating her claim that one's identity stems from never forgetting who they are.

The majority of the action takes place after they board their bus. African Americans had only recently won the right to sit wherever they pleased. Julian's sensitivity to this fact magnifies the impact of every statement and movement made on the bus. Once she sees that all the passengers are white, Julian's mother is quick to comment: "I see we have the bus to ourselves." This initiates an exchange of complaints about the close proximity of blacks on the buses—and about blacks in general—between the mother and two other ladies in the front of the bus. They also discuss Julian's nonexistent writing career, agreeing amongst themselves that it was not such a great leap from typewriter sales to writing.

As Julian angrily withdraws, O'Connor brings the reader into the "inner compartment" of his mind, where we are exposed to an even greater quantity of his contemptuous thoughts. O'Connor also exposes his pretentious, self-righteous slant on all the events around him. The reader remains in Julian's mind until the bus stops and an African-American man steps on, sitting down across from Julian and his mother. A lady who had been involved in conversation with Julian's mother reacts by moving from her seat to a place further back in the bus. Julian then moves across the aisle to sit in her place, next to the black man. Much to Julian's chagrin, the man does not seem to notice him, but Julian does derive satisfaction from the fact that his mother is noticeably disturbed by his behavior.

Julian escapes back into his head and begins to fantasize about the great "lesson" that he will teach his mother. He imagines that he will refuse to accompany her off of the bus, leaving her guessing as to whether he will return for her. He envisions befriending a "distinguished" African-American man and bringing him home for the evening. His fantasy continues to a hypothetical occasion when he would only be able to find an African-American doctor for his desperately ill mother. His fantasies culminate in the provocative thought of falling in love with a "suspiciously Negroid" woman.

When the bus stops again, Julian drifts back into reality to find an African-American woman and her little boy getting on the bus. After surveying the seating options, the woman sits next to Julian, and the little boy sits next to Julian's mother. Julian experiences pure joy upon realizing that this woman and his mother are wearing identical hats. "He could not believe that Fate had thrust upon his mother such a lesson," O'Connor writes. However, as Julian attempts to revel in his mother's outrage, he is soon dispirited by how quickly she seems to recover and see humor in the situation. She also focuses her attention on the woman's "cute" little boy. Julian can hardly bear to realize that the "lesson" seems to be lost upon her.

Throughout this sequence, Julian intermittently notes the black woman's frozen anger. "The woman was rumbling like a volcano about to become active," O'Connor tells us. The playful flirtation that goes on between her little boy, Carver, and Julian's mother only seems to feed her rage. Her repeated attempts to keep Carver from peering at Julian's smiling mother are unsuccessful.

As the bus nears Julian's mother's stop, Julian and the woman beside him reach for the cord at the same time, for the same stop. Julian is suddenly struck by the fear that his mother will attempt to offer the little boy some petty change after they all disembark. As they leave the bus, Julian's mother begins rummaging through her purse for a nickel to give the little boy. Julian pleads with her not to do it, but she is determined. Unable to find a nickel, she pulls out a shiny new penny, which she hurries to offer to the little boy. The infuriated woman turns around and delivers a fierce blow to Julian's mother, sending her crashing to the pavement. Before Julian fully comprehends what has taken place, the woman shouts, "He don't take nobody's pennies!" and then strides rapidly down the street.

Julian helps his mother up and immediately starts chastising her with statements such as, "I told you not to do that," and "I hope this teaches you a lesson." Without responding, his mother walks swiftly down the street in the wrong direction. Julian follows her, continuing his pompous lecture. Eventually, he stops her and realizes that her face has taken on a vastly different look. As he stares at her, she says "Tell Grandpa to come get me," then, "Tell Caroline to come get me," before limping a few more paces, then collapsing. The story ends with Julian running frantically down the street, screaming for help. O'Connor tells us that the darkness seems to draw him back toward her as he runs, "postponing from moment to moment his entry into the world of guilt and sorrow." ❀

List of Characters in
"Everything That Rises Must Converge"

Julian's mother has been instructed by her doctor to lose weight, so she attends a reducing class at the downtown Y. She is afraid to travel alone at night on the buses since they have been integrated, so she insists that her son accompany her. She places great value on dressing properly even to attend a reducing class, displaying a class-consciousness that evokes contempt from her son. She and Julian leave the bus at the same time as an African-American woman and her son. When Julian's mother attempts to offer a penny to the little boy, his mother strikes her down, and she dies of a stroke within minutes.

Julian is the son, who fancies himself liberal-minded and intellectually superior. O'Connor also characterizes him as a would-be writer with no real promise. He is filled with contempt toward his mother and is ashamed of her backward views on race and class. He accompanies his mother downtown on the bus and spends the majority of the ride fantasizing about the great civil rights lessons that he could teach her. When his mother is struck down by the enraged African-American lady, he unsympathetically scolds her. When she drops dead as a result of the blow, he is overcome with fear, and O'Connor tells us that "entry into the world of guilt and sorrow" awaits him.

The gaily dressed colored woman comes aboard the bus wearing a hat identical to Julian's mother's. She has her little boy, Carver, with her and she grows increasingly angry as Julian's mother playfully interacts with the child. When Julian's mother offers Carver a penny, the black woman turns around and strikes her. O'Connor also describes the gaily dressed woman as "sullen-looking."

Carver is the little African-American boy who sits next to Julian's mother. When Julian's mother offers him a penny, Carver's mother strikes her.

The large negro man is the first African American on the bus. He sits across from Julian and his mother. When the woman seated next to the black man moves, Julian takes her seat.

The woman with the protruding teeth is the first person with whom Julian's mother engages in conversation.

The woman with the red and white canvas sandals moves to another seat when the African-American man sits next to her. ❀

Critical Views on
"Everything That Rises Must Converge"

Carter W. Martin on O'Connor's Sacramental View

[Carter W. Martin (b. 1933) became a full-time professor of English at the University of Alabama, Huntsville, in 1971. He has been a member of the Modern Language Association of America and the Society for the Study of Southern Literature. In this excerpt from his book, *The True Country*, Martin discusses the element of redemption in O'Connor's fiction.]

The very title of her posthumously published volume of short stories, *Everything That Rises Must Converge*, expresses Flannery O'Connor's constant concern with man's "slow participation" in redemption. The title is taken from the writings of a Jesuit priest, Pierre Teilhard de Chardin, "whose works Flannery O'Connor had been reading at least since early 1961," and whose ideas are highly relevant to the particular meaning of Flannery O'Connor's sacramental view. Teilhard's *The Phenomenon of Man* expresses his belief in an evolutionary process toward an ultimate Omega point, at which the consciousness of the self (hominisation, "the individual and instantaneous leap from instinct to thought . . . [and] the progressive phyletic spiritualization in human civilization of all the forces contained in the animal world") is coincident with, but not contradictory to, an absorption into the Oneness of universal energy, both physical and psychical, which exists beyond the organic multiplicity of the past. Basing his opinions on biology, physics, archaeology—upon all fields of science—Teilhard demonstrates the existence of an evolutionary force in even the lowest forms of life driving them toward ever-increasing complexity, rising toward the phenomenon of man. Because space and time contain and engender consciousness, they are "necessarily *of a convergent nature*" and productive of higher forms of spiritual life.

Such ideas as Teilhard's may not on the surface seem appreciably different from those of Bergson or of Sir Julian Huxley, as Huxley himself points out in his introduction to *The Phenomenon of Man*; Teilhard in his preface to the same book asks that it be read as a scientific treatise and not as a theological essay or as a work on metaphysics. Yet he explains in the epilogue, "The Christian Phenomenon," that Christianity is the most potent manifestation of hominisation, of rising and convergence. In the essay itself he insists upon the importance in the scheme of individual, personal recognitions which contribute to the general upward movement of the phylum. The universe builds itself from thought, which moves in an upward direction, opposite to the movement of matter. "The universe is a collector and conservator, not of mechanical energy..., but of persons." Separate souls carry their consciousness upward but become synthesized at the Omega point, at which the convergent nature of the universe is achieved.

> —Carter W. Martin, *The True Country: Themes in the Fiction of Flannery O'Connor* (Nashville, TN: Vanderbilt University Press, 1969), pp. 15–17

PRESTON M. BROWNING, JR. ON O'CONNOR'S BOOK *EVERYTHING THAT RISES MUST CONVERGE*

[Preston M. Browning, Jr. teaches English and American literature at the University of Illinois, Chicago Circle. He completed his doctoral dissertation on the study of Flannery O'Connor's novels. In this excerpt from his book, *Flannery O'Connor*, Browning focuses on the stories contained in O'Connor's posthumous collection, *Everything That Rises Must Converge*.]

Like many of the sad young men of Flannery O'Connor's last stories, the protagonist of "Everything That Rises Must Converge" wants desperately to distinguish himself from everything in the South which he finds morally, intellectually, and aesthetically repugnant: its racism, its nostalgia for the glorious past, its (to him) petty concern with manners, its barren intellectual life, its insufferably banal social intercourse. (Julian is cast from the same mold that produced the rebellious "artistic" or "intellectual" sons of "The Enduring Chill," "The Comforts of Home," and "Greenleaf." Julian, Asbury, Thomas, and Wesley make up a quartet of angry, frustrated individuals caught in "late adolescent" impotence so acute that they can direct their hostility only against their protective, and oftentimes patronizing and controlling mothers.)

Julian wants to be different, and since everything about the South which affronts his sense of decency and decorum is symbolized by his mother, Julian wants especially to be different from his mother. Merely being different, however, is not sufficient; his hatred for all that his mother epitomizes is so venomous that he must constantly insult it. As it is impossible to insult the entire Southern ethos, Julian is reduced to the expediency of humiliating and insulting his mother. But Julian's relation to his mother, like his relation to the South itself, is less unambiguous than he would like to imagine. What he thinks he detests, he also loves and longs for. What he believes he is totally free of, he is, in fact, fearfully dependent upon.

While Miss O'Connor undoubtedly portrays the bad faith of Julian as the more damning, it must be conceded that there is something exasperating about his mother. She is one of those legendary Southern matrons of "aristocratic" birth who, though forced to live in relative poverty, continues to insist upon a distinction which she believes birth has conferred upon her. Though she must use the now-integrated public transportation system and must associate at the YWCA with women of a lower social class, she insists that because she "'knows who she is,'" she "'can be gracious to anybody.'" Indeed, it is this assumption that the glue which holds society together is a certain politeness and openness of manner—almost always, however, practiced with a degree of unconscious condescension—which enables Julian's mother to face the unpleasant alterations in her external circumstances with a calm and cheerful assurance that she herself at least has not changed. It is her ardent faith in the primacy of manners, in fact, which is one of the sources of the conflict between Julian and his mother. She insists that authentic culture is "'in the heart . . . and in how you do things and how you do things is because of who you *are*.'"

—Preston M. Browning, Jr., *Flannery O'Connor* (Carbondale and Edwardsville: Southern Illinois University Press, 1974), pp. 100–102

[Janet Egleson Dunleavy (b. 1928) became a professor at the
University of Wisconsin in 1976. She has edited many schol-
arly journals and books, including *George Moore in Perspective* (1983). In this essay, Dunleavy addresses the roles of
blacks and whites in O'Connor's short fiction.]

Less affluent than Asbury, Julian of "Everything That Rises Must
Converge" has not been able to support his image of himself as an
author by moving to such a two-room, five-floor walk-up in New
York, with garbage on each landing, that Asbury enjoyed, nor is he
able to boast of having worked alongside black farmhands in a dairy.
His apprenticeship in literary art has consisted of selling typewriters.
Nevertheless, he is as disdainful of the white Southerners around
him as Asbury, as eager to show the black Southerners he encounters
(when he accompanies his mother downtown on the bus, to the
exercise class ordered by the doctor to help control her high blood
pressure) that he does not share white Southern attitudes and values.
His greatest embarrassment is his mother, who persists in reminding
him that his great-grandfather had owned a plantation and two
hundred slaves; who reminisces about her own childhood when Caroline, "the old darky," was her nurse; and who commiserates with
other white passengers over the fact that the buses are now integrated. In retaliation Julian makes a point of sitting next to the first
Negro to board the bus and daydreams about calling a black doctor
to attend to his mother on her deathbed (or, better still, bringing her
to her deathbed by introducing a beautiful black woman as his
intended wife). Meanwhile a large sullen-looking black woman
boards the bus with a little boy and squeezes herself into the small
space next to Julian; the little boy clambers into the seat next to
Julian's mother and initiates the kind of flirtation often engaged in
by older women and small children. Julian's mother responds (to her
all children are cute) and, turning to the mother of the child, who
makes no attempt to conceal her irritation, she flashes "the smile she
used when she was being particularly gracious to an inferior." The
four dismount the bus at the same stop. As the black woman jerks
the boy toward her, Julian's mother, still smiling, offers the child a
penny. "He don't take nobody's pennies," shouts the woman, slap-
ping Julian's mother's outstretched arm with such force as to knock

her off balance (. Hauling his mother to her feet, Julian tells her that she got what she deserved: "Don't think that was just an uppity Negro woman ... That was the whole colored race which will no longer take your condescending pennies ... the old world is gone. The old manners are obsolete and your graciousness is not worth a damn." Without replying, his mother staggers along the sidewalk, muttering "Home"; "Tell Grandpa to come get me"; and then, before she collapses and dies on the pavement, "Tell Caroline to come get me."

—Janet Egleson Dunleavy, "A Particular History: Black and White in Flannery O'Connor's Short Fiction." In *Critical Essays on Flannery O'Connor*, eds. Melvin J. Friedman and Beverly Lyon Clark (Boston: G. K. Hall & Co., 1985), pp. 197–198

EDWARD KESSLER ON THE VIOLENCE OF METAPHOR IN O'CONNOR'S FICTION

[Edward Kessler (b. 1927) was a professor of literature at American University in Washington, D.C. His book *Images of Wallace Stevens* was chosen for "Scholar's Bookshelf" by the Modern Language Association of America in 1973. His other publications include *Night Thoughts* (poetry with engravings) (1973). In this excerpt from his book *Flannery O'Connor and the Language of Apocalypse*, Kessler addresses the violent use of metaphor in O'Connor's fiction.]

In "Everything That Rises Must Converge," O'Connor creates a situation in which social rituals, metaphorically represented by smiling, serve to bring about altered states of consciousness. The story belongs in the end to the young man Julian, who discovers the unsmiling nature of reality when his mother collapses, but the central plot concerns the encounter between his mother, a product of white supremacy, and a black woman whose smoldering resentment flares up in violence. In other O'Connor stories, smiles indicate that blacks accept stereotypical roles which demand gestures without genuine meaning—"The two of them came in grinning and shuffled to the side of the bed"—but in this anomalous story she questions whether facial expression can ever represent interior truth. By placing an angry Negro woman who rejects smiles of condescension next to Mrs. Chestney who grew up in an era when smiles promoted social harmony, though not racial equality, O'Connor approaches her true subject, which transcends topical issues.

Mrs. Chestney enters the bus as one enters one's *circle*, "with a little smile as if she were going into a drawing room where everyone has been waiting for her." Annoyed by his mother's ignorance of the current social situation, Julian takes a perverse pleasure in exposing what he sees as her hypocritical attitude toward black people. When his mother discovers that she and the black woman are wearing identical hats, Julian experiences satanic pleasure: "Justice entitled him to laugh. His grin hardened until it said to her as plainly as if he were saying it aloud: Your punishment exactly fits your pettiness." The justice without mercy behind Julian's grin contrasts with his mother's smiling at the Negro woman and her "grinning" child. But O'Connor in this story, advocates neither smile and, as usual in her stories, we need to be aware of who is interpreting facial or verbal expressions. Julian reports of his mother: "She kept her eyes on the woman and an amused smile came over her face *as if the woman were a monkey that had stolen her hat*" [my emphasis]. Julian interprets (reads his meaning into) his mother's smile and continues to explain her private emotions:

> "I think he likes me," Julian's mother said, and smiled at the woman.
>
> It was the smile she used when she was being particularly gracious to an inferior.

Not only does he know what lies behind his mother's expressions, he assumes a god-like knowledge of the mind and feelings of her black counterpart: "Julian could feel the rage in her at having no weapon like his mother's smile." O'Connor conveys the contempt (and cruelty) of Julian's smile, but his mother's condescension remains unproved, though perhaps real. However, even though Mrs. Chestney's consciousness may be corrupt, she does engage in human relations, whereas her son is like some Hawthorne character who discovers that seeing into the nature of sin is worse than sinning itself. O'Connor does not choose sides or express her personal views on racial integration; she is more concerned with the destructive power of selfishness and pride. She wrote to a friend: "The topical is poison. I got away with it in 'Everything That Rises' but only because I say a plague on everybody's house as far as the race business goes."

—Edward Kessler, *Flannery O'Connor and the Language of Apocalypse* (Princeton, NJ: Princeton University Press, 1986), pp. 42–44

JOHN F. DESMOND ON COMMUNITY AND HISTORY IN O'CONNOR'S FICTION

[John F. Desmond (b. 1939) became a professor of American literature at Whitman College, Walla Walla, Washington in 1975. His publications include *A Still Moment: Essays on the Art of Eudora Welty* (1978). In this excerpt from his book, *Risen Sons*, Desmond focuses on the historical element in O'Connor's fiction.]

O'Connor's most direct treatment of this historical process came in "Everything That Rises Must Converge," but here the emphasis is on the refusal to participate in that process and the terrible costs that refusal entails. The Teilhardian title specifically evokes the Christian idea of history as an evolutionary movement leading toward final "convergence" in a mystical community, but O'Connor's adaptation of the theme stresses humanity's capacity for rejecting cooperation with that process and for resisting transformation. Thus the story dramatizes the violent convergence of different visions of history and the self-inflicted spiritual violence suffered by those who resist accepting their identity within the corporate unity.

The view of history implicitly held by Julian's mother is retrogressive and in that respect it is similar to that of her "double" in the story, the large Negro woman on the bus. Regarding the blacks' drive for social equality, Julian's mother believes that "they should rise, but on their own side." Aristocratic and patronizing, her view is based upon her memory of a childhood in the old hierarchic South which she has romanticized into an image of order and stability. This view, of course, masks the true source of her dissociation from history: her underlying prideful belief in her own superiority separates her from any authentic involvement in the corporate process of change.

Though she prides herself on having adapted with dignity to social change, in fact she has resisted true association at every turn.

Her condition is ironically underscored by the key images of transformation in the story—mock transformation, that is—such as the "reduced circumstances" that she and Julian now find themselves in and her attendance in a reducing class at the YMCA, as if transformation were simply a question of physical fitness. The truth, of course, is that she has not essentially changed at all, a fact demonstrated by her spiritual "return" to childhood after being struck by the Negro woman. She regresses to what she has always been, a child linked to the aristocratic Chestneys and Godhighs, as in dying she calls for her grandfather and her maid to take her "home." This regression is appropriate in the sense of being retribution for her presumptuous dissociation from the reality of history; more significantly, it is a return to the only starting point in "childhood" from which any true spiritual growth might possibly begin.

—John F. Desmond, *Risen Sons: Flannery O'Connor's Vision of History* (Athens: The University of Georgia Press, 1987), pp. 68–69

MARSHALL BRUCE GENTRY ON GENDER DIALOGUE IN O'CONNOR'S FICTION

[Marshall Bruce Gentry (b. 1953) teaches American literature and the short story at the University of Indianapolis. His publications include *Conversations with Raymond Carver* (1990). In this essay, Gentry analyzes the gender dialogue in O'Connor's fiction.]

These two clearly ridiculous narrators, the farm wife Mrs. P. and Miss Willerton, are, of course, both women, and when I in the past have described an O'Connor character as a version of the typical O'Connor narrator, that character was another female, Sarah Ruth Cates from "Parker's Back." This woman disapproves of cars and even considers "churches . . . idolatrous"; like the typical O'Connor narrator, she is "forever sniffing up sin." Robert H. Brinkmeyer, Jr., however, has pointed to a male character, Julian in "Everything That Rises Must Converge," as one who resembles the O'Connor narrator: "In their efforts to show people up, both Julian and the narrator distort and demean; they manipulate to teach a lesson, simplifying the complexity of human experience to validate their own—but no one else's—integrity. A central irony of the story lies in this mirroring of Julian and the narrator, for because of their close identification, Julian's downfall implicitly signals the narrator's even if the narrator remains unaware of it."

Most of O'Connor's writers are male, and most of her writers receive ridicule; along with Julian, one thinks of Asbury Fox in "The Enduring Chill," Thomas in "The Comforts of Home," Calhoun in "The Partridge Festival" (though Calhoun does have a female counterpart, Mary Elizabeth), and Rayber in *The Violent Bear It Away*. But O'Connor's women also frequently tell stories, orally rather than in writing. The issue of whether the typical O'Connor narrator is male or female can be resolved, I believe, through the positing of a composite figure: a female narrator espousing patriarchal, masculine values.

I should provide an explanation about the narration in the stories I have been discussing. I do not wish to claim that Miss Willerton dialogically rivals her narrator for authority in "The Crop"; I consider Miss Willerton as much of a joke as Ruth Fennick does. Miss Willerton's failure to win the reader's sympathy is one reason this story looks like an apprentice story. In "Everything That Rises Must Converge," the narrator resembles a woman as much as a man. The narrator's satire is like a lightning bolt of judgment delivered by the black mother who hits and perhaps kills Julian's mother for patronizing the black child.

—Marshall Bruce Gentry, "Gender Dialogue in O'Connor." In *Flannery O'Connor: New Perspectives*, eds. Sura P. Rath and Mary Neff Shaw (Athens, GA: The University of Georgia Press, 1996), pp. 59–60

Plot Summary of
"Revelation"

"Revelation," the final story published separately before O'Connor's death in the summer of 1964, is considered by many critics to be her finest. The story opens in a doctor's waiting room, just as the Turpins (Mrs. Ruby Turpin and her husband, Claud) enter. The waiting room is very small, in contrast to Mrs. Turpin's considerable girth, and there is only one vacant seat, which she instructs her husband to take. Mrs. Turpin explains to whoever will listen that her husband has an ulcer on his leg where a cow kicked him. Eventually, someone is called into the doctor's office and Mrs. Turpin finds a seat.

Once Mrs. Turpin is seated, the story's action takes the form of a conversation between Mrs. Turpin and the well-dressed "pleasant lady"—with interjections from a slovenly "white-trash woman," who is accompanied by a gaunt old woman and a dirty, lethargic child. O'Connor also makes us continually aware of the silent, acned, and obese teenage girl (the pleasant lady's daughter) who periodically peers up from behind her "thick blue book," entitled *Human Development,* to scowl at Mrs. Turpin. In addition to the content of the conversation, the reader hears the judgmental inner voice of Mrs. Turpin. The labels she assigns to the other characters in the waiting room are the only names that O'Connor gives them (with the exception of the ugly girl, whose name is Mary Grace). We also learn that Mrs. Turpin will occasionally "occupy herself with the question of who she would have chosen to be if she couldn't be herself," if the options were "either a nigger or white-trash." O'Connor tells us that after begging Jesus for some other alternative, Mrs. Turpin would have said, "All right, make me a nigger then." Mrs. Turpin also occupies some of her time "naming the classes of people," placing herself and Claud near the top because of the color of their skin and the fact that they are "home-and-land owners."

The waiting-room conversation seems fairly generic, with topics ranging from clocks to picking cotton, each subject prompting the ladies involved to make statements that immediately fall under Mrs. Turpin's private scrutiny. When the white-trash woman chimes in about green stamps, saying that she redeemed hers for "some joo'ry", Mrs. Turpin snipes inwardly, "Ought to have got you a wash rag and some soap." It is not until the topic turns to pigs and African-American help that we have a mild verbal confrontation between Mrs. Turpin and the trashy woman, creating a tension which resurfaces periodically throughout the remainder of the waiting room scene. The room becomes quiet following the brief appearance of an African-American delivery boy. This silence is broken by the white-trash, who believes "They ought to send all them niggers back to Africa."

As the tension between the ladies in the waiting room momentarily rises, O'Connor keeps us updated on the ugly girl, who has been flashing Mrs. Turpin malevolent looks throughout the scene. Mrs. Turpin, in turn, has registered her private pity for the girl's foul looks and disposition. She has also figured out that this girl is the pleasant lady's daughter. To help ease the tension, the pleasant lady asks the white-trash woman about her son. As she talks about her little boy's ulcer, we drift back into Mrs. Turpin's head, where we are treated to her condescending internal diatribe about white trash and their inability to help themselves. "There was nothing you could tell her about people like them that she didn't know already," O'Connor writes. Mrs. Turpin then becomes acutely aware of the teenage girl's agitated glare. To overcome her intimidation, she looks directly at the girl and tries to engage her in a conversation about college. "The girl continued to stare and pointedly did not answer," O'Connor tells us. Embarrassed by her daughter's insolence, the pleasant lady takes the liberty of explaining that her daughter studies at Wellesley College, and mentioning, much to the girl's displeasure, that she is concerned about her daughter's limited social life.

This tangent leads to a fairly lengthy discussion about "bad dispositions," instigated by the pleasant lady in a none-too-subtle attempt to comment upon her daughter. Mrs. Turpin feels compelled to "thank the Lord" that she has been blessed with a good disposition. The pleasant lady continues to make indirect remarks about her daughter, commenting on how awful it is when people are not grateful. Mrs. Turpin seizes this opportunity to praise her own grateful nature. She proceeds to praise Jesus—out loud as well as in her head— for all she has been given. "Flooded with gratitude," she finally cries out, "Oh thank you Jesus, Jesus, thank you!" which pushes the infuriated girl over the edge. She heaves her big blue book at Mrs. Turpin's head and hurls herself on top of her, howling and sinking her fingers into Mrs. Turpin's neck.

The girl is quickly pulled off of Mrs. Turpin and injected with a sedative. As Mrs. Turpin attempts to regain her composure, she gazes into Mary Grace's eyes and is struck by the feeling that the girl "knew her in some intense and personal way, beyond time and place and condition." She turns to the girl, who is lying on the floor, and says, "What you got to say to me?" The girl responds by fixing her eyes directly on Mrs. Turpin and saying in a low voice, "Go back to hell where you came from, you old wart hog."

An ambulance carries the girl away, and the doctor examines both of the Turpins. They return home and retire to their bed. Claud quickly falls asleep, leaving Mrs. Turpin awake and haunted by the girl's words. She at first tearfully denies that she is a "wart hog from hell," then grows angry. She is outraged that she, "a respectable, hard-working, church-going woman," was called such a name.

That evening, Claud leaves the house to pick up their hired hands. Mrs. Turpin remains in bed until she hears "the pick-up truck coming back with the Negroes." Putting on her clothes, she carries a bucket of ice water down to the truck, as she always does, and greets the workers. Upon seeing her bruised face, the workers inquire about her condition. After hearing all about the office and the girl and the book, the workers express their disbelief and attempt to cheer her up with compliments about her sweetness and prettiness. "Mrs. Turpin knew exactly how much Negro flattery was worth and it added to her rage," writes O'Connor. Her anger prompts her to blurt out that she had been called "a wart hog from hell." The workers' sympathy strikes her as idiotic, and Mrs. Turpin stalks off, clenched with rage.

Mrs. Turpin walks to her pig parlor where she starts hosing down the hogs. This naturally brings back the words of the white-trash woman, who had continually expressed her disgust at pigs, with their "a-gruntin and a-rootin and a-groanin." Looking at his wife's irritated expression, Claud remarks, "You look like you might have swallowed a mad dog," before heading back to his truck.

Mrs. Turpin remains in the parlor and asks God out loud how she could be a hog and herself at the same time. "How am I saved and from hell too?" she asks in a demanding tone. She hoses down her pigs roughly as she rails at her creator with increasing sarcasm. "A final surge of fury shook her," O'Connor writes, "and she roared, 'Who do you think you are?'" Soon after her outburst, she sees a "visionary light" shooting up toward heaven. Upon this light she sees a group of souls—comprised of the various inferior groups that Mrs. Turpin had identified in her mind—rising into heaven. People "like herself and Claud" trail behind "whole companies of white-trash, clean for the first time in their lives, and bands of black niggers in white robes, and battalions of freaks and lunatics shouting and clapping and leaping like frogs." The story ends as the vision fades and the chirping of crickets echoes from the woods, manifesting itself in Mrs. Turpin's mind as "the voices of the souls climbing upward into the starry field and shouting hallelujah." ❀

List of Characters in
"Revelation"

Mrs. Ruby Turpin is the first character O'Connor introduces and the story is told from her perspective. She is portrayed as a very talkative and fairly obese woman. She makes judgments in her head about the types of people that are in the waiting room. It becomes noticeable that a college-age girl in the room is repulsed by her. As Mrs. Turpin loudly praises Jesus for all that she has been blessed with, the girl attacks her. Mrs. Turpin becomes haunted by the girl's private message to her, in which she calls Mrs. Turpin an old wart hog from hell. Working at her pig parlor later that day, Mrs. Turpin has a vision of the various classes of people represented in the waiting room—and other types of people she categorizes as inferior— rising to heaven and shouting hallelujah.

Mr. Claud Turpin is Mrs. Turpin's good-humored husband, whose ulcerated leg brings them to the doctor's office. He is driving the black hired hands home from the field when Mrs. Turpin has her vision.

The pleasant lady is the mother of Mary Grace, the college-age girl who attacks Mrs. Turpin. She is a primary contributor to the waiting room conversation and is depicted as the woman of highest social standing according to Mrs. Turpin's appraisal.

Mary Grace is the 18- or 19-year-old daughter of the pleasant lady. She reads a large book entitled *Human Development* and periodically scowls at Mrs. Turpin throughout most of the waiting room scene. At the end of the waiting room scene, she attacks Mrs. Turpin, gets injected with a sedative, and is hauled off to the hospital—but not before telling Mrs. Turpin to go back to hell and calling her an old wart hog.

The white-trash woman is at the doctor's office with her son and the boy's grandmother and is a primary, if unwelcome, contributor to the waiting room conversation. Mrs. Turpin makes incessant mental comments about the slovenly nature of the white-trash woman.

The colored delivery boy appears briefly to drop something off at the doctor's office. His appearance instigates a conversation about integration and the feasibility of sending blacks back to Africa.

The hired hands are the Turpins' African-American cotton field workers. They speak with Mrs. Turpin after the incident at the doctor's office and they try to flatter her with unappreciated compliments. They are riding home in the back of Claud's truck when Mrs. Turpin has her vision. ✿

Critical Views on
"Revelation"

SISTER M. BERNETTA QUINN, O. S. F., ON O'CONNOR
AS A REALIST OF DISTANCES

[Sister M. Bernetta Quinn, O. S. F. (b. 1915), entered the
Order of St. Francis in 1934. She has been involved in prison
rehabilitation work and has taught at various institutions
including Andrew's Presbyterian College. Her publications
include *Dancing in Stillness* (1982). In this essay, Quinn discusses justice and categorizes O'Connor as a realist.]

"Revelation," one of the very last stories, shows that Flannery
O'Connor believed in justice, not racial justice, as the best way of
handling questions of prejudice in the South. In a letter written
about a month before she died she said:

> Justice is justice and should not be appealed to along racial lines. The
> problem is not abstract for the Southerner, it's concrete; he sees it in
> terms of persons, not races—which way of seeing does away with
> easy answers. I have tried to touch this subject by way of fiction only
> once—in a story called "Everything That Rises Must Converge."

The prophecy in the story referred to in the letter is not directly concerned with the Negro woman and her son but rather with Julian's
relationship to his mother. In "Revelation," however, written after
this, she uses prophecy to bring out her insistence on true charity if
races are to live together in peace. Complacent people seem especially to have annoyed Flannery O'Connor.

Mrs. Turpin, the leading character, is such a person. In view of all
her virtues, she simply cannot understand how Jesus could let a
lunatic girl publicly prophesy to her: "Go back to hell where you came
from, you old wart hog." Once home, obsessed by the incident, she
tries to get rid of her irritation by hosing down the pig parlor, but the
sun stares at her out of a fiery sunset, like a farmer inspecting his own
hogs. The dying light takes on the figuration of a path into eternity:

She raised her hands from the side of the pen in a gesture hieratic and profound. A visionary light settled in her eyes. She saw the streak as a vast swinging bridge extending upward from the earth through a field of living fire. Upon it a vast horde of souls were rumbling toward heaven. There were whole companies of white-trash, clean for the first time in their lives, and bands of black niggers in white robes, and battalions of freaks and lunatics shouting and clapping and leaping like frogs. And bringing up the end of the procession was a tribe of people whom she recognized at once as those who, like herself and Claud [her husband], had always had a little of everything and the God-given wit to use it right. She leaned forward to watch them closer. They were marching behind the others with great dignity, accountable as they had always been for good order and common sense and respectable behavior. They all were on one key. Yet she could see by their shocked and altered faces that even their virtues were being burned away.

All along in the novella, the writer has been underscoring Saint Paul's warning that the greatest of virtues is charity. Mrs. Turpin's attitude toward her husband's Negro employees shows how far she is from practicing charity. What has appeared to her throughout life to be virtue is really selfishness. What Mrs. Turpin does with this revelation the story does not say.

—Sister M. Bernetta Quinn, O. S. F., "Flannery O'Connor, a Realist of Distances." In *The Added Dimension: The Art and Mind of Flannery O'Connor,* eds. Melvin J. Friedman and Lewis A. Lawson (New York: Fordham University Press, 1966), pp. 176–177

RONALD SCHLEIFER ON THE STORIES OF FLANNERY O'CONNOR

[Ronald Schleifer (b. 1948) is a professor of English at the University of Oklahoma. He has been the editor of the *Genre* publication since 1976. His publications include *A. J. Greimas and the Nature of Meaning: Linguistics, Semiotics and Discourse Theory* (1987) and *Rhetoric and Death: The Language of Modernism and Post Modern Discourse Theory*

(1990). In this essay, Schleifer addresses the rural gothic element in O'Connor's stories.]

Such confrontations with the literal—the literal self, its literal origin, a literal meaning—are the repeated actions in Flannery O'Connor, and they take place in what John Hawkes has called "her almost luridly bright pastoral world," on borderlines between the city and the country or between day and night. This is why so often O'Connor's stories end at sunset, as in "Revelation," when Mrs. Turpin watches her hogs as the sun goes down:

> Then like a monumental statue coming to life, she bent her head slowly and gazed, as if through the very heart of mystery, down into the pig parlor at the hogs. They had settled all in one corner around the old sow who was grunting softly. A red glow suffused them. They appeared to pant with a secret life.

From this sight she looks up as the sun goes down and sees her vision of a vast horde of souls going to heaven, "whole companies of white-trash, clean for the first time in their lives, and bands of black niggers in white robes, and battalions of freaks and lunatics shouting and clapping and leaping like frogs." The metaphor O'Connor uses is almost an allusion to *Otranto* with its giant statue coming to life, but the language is that of Mrs. Turpin, another in O'Connor's procession of good country people. That language informs a rural vision, Hawkes's lurid pastoral world, with a sense of supernatural force so that the whole is seen in a new light. Here again O'Connor creates the *presence* of the super-natural, of mysterious forces beyond the daylight self, in pig and sunset. "Revelation" begins with Mrs. Turpin's confrontation with a Wellesley student in a doctor's office, yet it ends with her own uncouthness—her own rural sensibility—miraculously trans-formed in the presence of a secret life.

That life is Mrs. Turpin's life, but dark, unknown, strange: it is the life revealed in the college girl's fierce remark: "Go back to hell where you came from, you old wart hog." It is the inhuman life of wart hogs from hell that, literalized, leads strangely to Mrs. Turpin's vision of heaven. Mrs. Turpin "faces" herself with the hog; she sees her own secret life in the elemental life of her farm and discovers, as Parker had, the presence of God in and beyond His creation, in and beyond the hogs, the people, the peculiar light of the setting sun.

—Ronald Schleifer, "Rural Gothic: The Stories of Flannery O'Connor." In *Critical Essays on Flannery O'Connor*, eds. Melvin J. Friedman and Beverly Lyon Clark (Boston: G. K. Hall & Co., 1985), p. 164

MICHAEL GRESSET ON THE AUDACITY OF FLANNERY O'CONNOR

[Michael Gresset is a professor of English at the Institut d'Anglais, Universita de Paris VII. His publications include *Fascination: Faulkner's Fiction, 1919–1936* (1989). In this essay, Gresset addresses O'Connor's sense of the connection between art and faith.]

This gives rise to a question that is difficult to resolve without making an a priori judgment in one direction or the other: how is art indebted to faith? One knows that Flannery O'Connor was a fervent Catholic (in a Protestant country). An attempt to dissociate art and faith in her work has already been made. But, after what has been said, it would seem that the answer is bound to the problem posed thus: what is the content of Flannery O'Connor's revelations?

Such a question is best served by looking at a passage where the narrative explicitly displays (something that is rare) the precise phenomenon of a vision. This occurs at the end of "Revelation." In the waiting room of a country doctor, Mrs. Turpin, who is accompanying her husband, Claud ("Florid and bald and sturdy, somewhat shorter than Mrs. Turpin, but he sat down as if he were accustomed to doing what she told him to"), after an extraordinary dialogue made up of displays of self-contentment and shared opinions with a neighbor, has been literally attacked by a pimply student from Wellesley, an ugly girl whose name happens to be Mary Grace and who has hurled at her, along with her book entitled *Human Development,* this insult: "Go back to hell where you came from, you old wart hog." After going home in a traumatic state, Mrs. Turpin meditates on her pigsty, the pigs suffused with a red glow and seeming "to pant with a secret life"; she lifts her head and

> There was only a purple streak in the sky, cutting through a field of crimson and leading, like an extension of the highway, into the descending dusk. She raised her hands from the side of the pen in a gesture hieratic and profound. A visionary light settled in her eyes. She saw the streak as a vast swinging bridge extending upward from the earth through a field of living fire. Upon it a vast horde of souls were rumbling toward heaven. There were whole companies of white-trash, clean for the first time in their lives, and bands of black niggers in white robes, and battalions of freaks and lunatics shouting and clapping and leaping like frogs. And bringing up the end of the procession was a tribe of people whom she recognized at once as those who, like herself and Claud, had always had a little of everything and the God-given wit to use it right. She leaned forward to observe them closer. They were marching behind the others with great dignity, accountable as they had always been for good order and common sense and respectable behavior. They alone were on key. Yet she could see by their shocked and altered faces that even their virtues were being burned away. She lowered her hands and gripped the rail of the hog pen, her eyes small but fixed unblinkingly on what lay ahead.

> —Michael Gresset, "The Audacity of Flannery O'Connor." In *Critical Essays on Flannery O'Connor*, eds. Melvin J. Friedman and Beverly Lyon Clark (Boston: G. K. Hall & Co., 1985), pp. 104–105

RICHARD POIRIER ON O'CONNOR'S FICTION

[Richard Poirier (b. 1925) was named chair of the advisory committee on English at Harvard University. He has been director of graduate studies at Rutgers University since 1970. In 1981, he founded and became acting editor of *Raritan: A Quarterly Review*. His publications include *Poetry and Pragmatism* (1992). In this essay, Poirier discusses pride in O'Connor's characters.]

Humility in the claims made for oneself, for what one knows and values, is in fact the operative standard within the stories. Pride makes a fool at some time or other of nearly all of her characters. It gets expressed not grandly but within the grotesqueries of daily, mostly Southern life, and within simple people who are aware of no alternatives to that life, once pride is destroyed, except death or a strange God.

Everything that rises must indeed converge, joining the anonymity either of oblivion or the blessed. The pride of her characters may be for a new hat, a bit of money, a college degree or clean hogs; it is her particular genius to make us believe that there are Christian mysteries in things irreducibly banal. And in this too there is an aspect of Catholicism, most beautifully exemplified in the penultimate stanza of the "Paradiso," where Dante likens his poetic efforts in fashioning a vision of God to the work of a "good tailor."

Her characters seem damned precisely to the degree that they lack Miss O'Connor's own "measure" of their trivialities. They have no measure for them but pride, and they can therefore appeal for authority only to mundane standards that never threaten it, to platitudes and to prejudices, very often racial ones. Necessarily, she is a mordantly comic writer. She offers us the very sounds of platitude ("If you know who you are you can go anywhere," remarks the mother to her intellectualist son in the title story), or of prejudice (as in the imagined dialogue with God of the pretentious lady in "Revelation," who would have asked Him to make her anything but white trash: "'All right make me a nigger, then—but that don't mean a trashy one.' And he would have made her a neat clean respectable Negro woman, herself but black.")

Except for sloth, pride is of all human failings the one that can be most difficult for a writer to translate into actions. Most often it expresses itself in a smugness of inaction, the hostilities it creates in others being the result merely of the tones of voice, the gestures, the placidities which are its evidence. Miss O'Connor can produce as much violence from a quiet conversation as can other writers from the confrontations of gangsters or fanatics, though she can manage that too.

The action in the best of these stories, "Revelation," is to a large extent dialogue, in which the veritable sounds of people talking gently in a doctor's office about everything from the heat to the ingratitude of children leads to a sudden but somehow expected flare-up of violence and disaster. With very little room for maneuver—most of her stories are about 20 pages long—she achieves transitions and even reversals of tone with remarkable speed, and she can show in people who have been almost preposterously flat a sudden visionary capacity. This absolute sureness of timing is, I think, what makes the reader assent to the religious directions which her stories take: from involvement in the most common stuff they move toward the Heaven and the Hell weirdly apprehended by her characters.

—Richard Poirier, "If You Know Who You Are You Can Go Anywhere." In *Critical Essays on Flannery O'Connor*, eds. Melvin J. Friedman and Beverly Lyon Clark (Boston: G. K. Hall & Co., 1985), pp. 45–46

JILL P. BAUMGAERTNER ON A PROPER SCARING IN THE FICTION OF FLANNERY O'CONNOR

[Jill P. Baumgaertner is a professor of English at Wheaton College. Baumgaertner did her dissertation work on the seventeenth-century poet John Donne. Her book *Flannery O'Connor: A Proper Scaring* was published in 1988. In this chapter, Baumgaertner discusses the extremes to which O'Connor takes her characters when leading them to revelations.]

For Mrs. Turpin in the story "Revelation," O'Connor prescribes less drastic measures. The story opens in a doctor's waiting room with a gospel hymn playing faintly in the background—a hymn to which Mrs. Turpin mentally supplies the words. She knows the forms of religion, she would probably talk freely about her personal relationship with Jesus, but she does not realize that she shares with the rest of Christendom a double identity—as both saint and sinner. Mrs. Turpin is most comfortable with clear definitions, with distinct, unambiguous categories. She tries to avoid thinking about people who do not fit neatly into her preconceived system of social hierarchy.

Sometimes Mrs. Turpin occupied herself at night naming the classes of people. On the bottom of the heap were most colored people, not the kind she would have been if she had been one, but most of them; then next to them—not above, just away from—were the white-trash; then above them were the home-owners, and above them the home-and-land owners, to which she and Claud belonged. Above she and Claud were people with a lot of money and much bigger houses and much more land. But here the complexity of it would begin to bear in on her, for some of the people with a lot of money were common and ought to be below she and Claud and some of the people who had good blood had lost their money and had to rent and then there were colored people who owned their homes and had to rent and then there were colored people who owned their homes and land as well. There was a colored dentist in town who had two red Lincolns and a swimming pool and a farm with registered white-face cattle on it. Usually by the time she had fallen asleep all the classes of people were moiling and roiling around in her head, and she would dream they were all crammed in together in a box car, being ridden off to be put in a gas oven.

The emblematic moment in this story occurs as Mrs. Turpin sits in the waiting room, praying self-righteous prayers of thanksgiving to Jesus for giving her such a good disposition. Abruptly, Mary Grace, a college student whose well-dressed mother has been speaking with Mrs. Turpin, throws a book (titled *Human Development*) at Mrs. Turpin and then attempts to strangle her. In the middle of her "Thank you, Jesus, Jesus, thank you," the book hits Mrs. Turpin above her left eye. God's intervention could not be more clear. While Mary Grace is being restrained and sedated, Mrs. Turpin leans over the girl and asks her what she has to say, "waiting, as for a revelation." Mary Grace answers, "Go back to hell where you came from, you old wart hog."

—Jill P. Baumgaertner, *Flannery O'Connor: A Proper Scaring* (Wheaton, IL: Harold Shaw Publishers, 1988), pp. 114–115

[Patricia Yaeger teaches English at the University of Michigan. Her publications include *Honey-Mad Women: Emancipatory Strategies in Women's Writing* (1988). In this essay, Yaeger discusses the role of torture in O'Connor's fiction.]

Although O'Connor bruises her characters to bring them to grace, she also uses these characters to disabuse us of the value of the southern cult of beauty. Her stories reveal a litany of ugly women— Sally Cope from "A Circle in the Fire," Joy/Hulga Hopewell from "Good Country People," Mary Grace from "Revelation"—who refuse to be socialized into pale southern beauties. Each of these characters tells a bitter story of gendered anger; their lives are filled with hateful emotions unacceptable to a southern lady.

In this context, it is tempting to rewrite O'Connor's tortured texts as angry feminist legends. Writing in a culture that refuses women their rage and intelligence, O'Connor uses both; like Mary Grace she throws the book at a southern world in which women are not allowed to be angry, ill-mannered, intelligent, or visionary. In cutting her characters, she usurps white male turf; she appropriates the cruel role of the patriarchal God of the Old Testament to foment her own cruelties. But we limit the terror of O'Connor's aggression if we stop here, if we simply read her stories as angry solutions to southern white women's plight as cultural victims. If the white female body can serve as an intensifying grid for the depravities of southern patriotism, it is because this body also becomes a reservoir for the worst compulsions of southern racism. "No I can't see James Baldwin in Georgia," O'Connor writes to Maryat Lee. "It would cause the greatest trouble and disturbance and disunion. In New York it would be nice to meet him; here it would not." Although her stories explore this disturbance and disunion, O'Connor was wary of the tempestuous racial politics of her time. Her letter to Maryat Lee was written in 1959, a time of extraordinary upheaval in the South. Three years earlier, when African Americans refused to ride segregated buses in Montgomery, their boycott ended in triumph when the Supreme Court ordered city officials to desegregate. But the South O'Connor inhabited in the 1950s and 1960s was still ruled by Jim Crow. In 1960 the Greensboro, North Carolina, lunch counter sit-ins ignited a widespread protest movements among black students that had no discernible impact on segregationists, while 1961 witnessed horrifying scenes of cruelty as black and white freedom riders were brutally attacked by white mobs. O'Connor lived in a region that thrilled to racist violence and danger. The white southerners of her era struggled to enforce sharp demarcations between genders, classes, and, most viciously, between races.

—Patricia Yaeger, "Flannery O'Connor and the Aesthetics of Torture." In *Flannery O'Connor: New Perspectives,* eds. Sura P. Rath and Mary Neff Shaw (Athens, GA: The University of Georgia Press, 1996), pp. 198–199

Books by
Flannery O'Connor

Wise Blood. 1952.

A Good Man Is Hard to Find. 1955.

The Violent Bear It Away. 1960.

Everything That Rises Must Converge. 1965.

Mystery and Manners (an edited selection of prose taken from lectures and essays). 1969.

The Collected Stories of Flannery O'Connor. 1971.

The Habit of Being (an edited selection of letters). 1979.

Works about Flannery O'Connor

Asals, Frederick. "The Double in Flannery O'Connor's Stories." *Flannery O'Connor Bulletin* 9 (1980): 49–84.

———. *Flannery O'Connor: The Imagination of Extremity.* Athens: University of Georgia Press, 1982.

Babinec, Lisa S. "Cyclical Patterns of Domination and Manipulation in Flannery O'Connor's Mother-Daughter Relationships." *Flannery O'Connor Bulletin* 19 (1990): 9–29.

Bacon, Jon Lance. *Flannery O'Connor and the Cold War Culture.* New York: Cambridge University Press, 1993.

Balee, Susan. *Flannery O'Connor: Literary Prophet of the South.* New York: Chelsea House Publishers, 1995.

Barcus, Nancy B. "Psychological Determinism and Freedom in Flannery O'Connor." *Cithara* 12.1 (1972): 26–33.

Blackwell, Louise. "Flannery O'Connor's Literary Style." *Antigonish Review* 10 (1972): 57–66.

Bliven, Naomi. Review of *Everything That Rises Must Converge*, by Flannery O'Connor. *New Yorker*, 2 September 1965, 220–21.

Brinkmeyer, Robert H., Jr. *The Art and Vision of Flannery O'Connor.* Baton Rouge: Louisiana State University Press, 1989.

Butler, Rebecca. "What's So Funny About Flannery O'Connor?" *Flannery O'Connor Bulletin* 9 (1980): 30–40.

Chew, Martha. "Flannery O'Connor's Double-Edged Satire: The Idiot Daughter Versus the Lady Ph.D." *Southern Quarterly* 19.2 (1981): 17–25.

Crews, Frederick. "The Power of Flannery O'Connor." *New York Review of Books*, 26 April 1990, 49–55.

Detweiler, Robert. "The Curse of Christ in Flannery O'Connor's Fiction." *Comparative Literature Studies* 3 (1966): 235–45.

Eggenschwiler, David. *The Christian Humanism of Flannery O'Connor.* Detroit, MI: Wayne State University Press, 1972.

Farmer, David. *Flannery O'Connor: A Descriptive Bibliography.* New York: Garland, 1981.

Feeley, Kathleen. *Flannery O'Connor: Voice of the Peacock.* New York: Fordham University Press, 1982.

Fitzgerald, Sally R. "The Country Side and the True Country." *Sewanee Review* 70 (1962): 380–94.

Friedman, Melvin J. "Flannery O'Connor: Another Legend in Southern Fiction." *English Journal* 51.4 (1962): 233–43.

Gentry, Marshall Bruce. *Flannery O'Connor's Religion of the Grotesque.* Jackson: University Press of Mississippi, 1986.

———. "Flannery O'Connor's Attacks on Omniscience." *Southern Quarterly* 29.3 (1991) 53–61.

Giannone, Richard. *Flannery O'Connor and the Mystery of Love.* Urbana: University of Illinois Press, 1989.

Hawkes, John. "Flannery O'Connor's Devil." *Sewanee Review 70* (1962): 395–407.

Hendin, Josephine. *The World of Flannery O'Connor.* Bloomington: Indiana University Press, 1970.

Howe, Irving, ed. "Flannery O'Connor's Stories." Review of *Everything That Rises Must Converge,* by Flannery O'Connor. *New York Review of Books,* 30 September, 1965.

Ingram, Forrest L. "O'Connor's Seven Story Cycle." *Flannery O'Connor Bulletin* 2 (1973): 19–28.

Jeremy, Sister. "The Comic Ritual of Flannery O'Connor." *Catholic Library World* 39 (1967): 195–200.

Leitch, Vincent B. *American Literary Criticism From the Thirties to the Eighties.* New York: Columbia University Press, 1988.

Maida, Patricia C. "Light and Enlightenment in Flannery O'Connor's Fiction." *Studies in Short Fiction* 13 (1976): 31–36.

May, John R. "Flannery O'Connor and the New Hermeneutic." *Flannery O'Connor Bulletin* 2 (1973): 29–42.

Montgomery, Marion. "Cloaks and Hats and Doubling in Poe and Flannery O'Connor." *South Carolina Review* 2 (1979): 60–69.

Muller, Gilbert H. *Nightmares and Visions: Flannery O'Connor and the Catholic Grotesque.* Athens: University of Georgia Press, 1972.

Nisly, Paul W. "Prison of the Self: Isolation in Flannery O'Connor's Fiction." *Studies in Short Fiction* 17 (1980): 49–54.

Orvell, Miles. *Invisible Parade: The Fiction of Flannery O'Connor.* Philadelphia: Temple University Press, 1972.

Ragen, Brian. "The Motions of Grace: Flannery O'Connor's Typology." (Ph.D. diss., Princeton University, 1987).

Rubin, Louis D., Jr. "Flannery O'Connor: A Note on Literary Fashions." *Critique* 2 (1985): 11–18.

Shinn, Thelma J. "Flannery O'Connor and the Violence of Grace." *Contemporary Literature* 9 (1968): 58–73.

Shloss, Carol. *Flannery O'Connor's Dark Comedies: The Limits of Inference.* Baton Rouge: Louisiana State University Press, 1980.

Spivey, Ted R. "Flannery O'Connor, the New Criticism and Deconstruction." *Southern Review* 23 (Spring 1987): 271–80.

Stephens, Martha. *The Question of Flannery O'Connor.* Baton Rouge: Louisiana University Press, 1973.

Tate, J. O. "The Essential Essex." *Flannery O'Connor Bulletin* 12 (1983): 47–59.

Westarp, Karl-Heinz. *Flannery O'Connor: The Growing Craft.* Birmingham, AL: Summa, 1993.

Whitt, Margaret. "Flannery O'Connor's Ladies." *Flannery O'Connor Bulletin* 15 (1986): 42–50.

Wynne, Judith F. "The Sacramental Irony of Flannery O'Connor." *Southern Literary Journal* 7, No. 2 (Spring 1975): 33–49.

Index of
Themes and Ideas

Christian Jr./Sr High School
2100 Greenfield Dr
El Cajon, CA 92019